MW01069761

Southside Buddhist

IRA SUKRUNGRUANG

Southside Buddhist

☙

ESSAYS

UNIVERSITY OF TAMPA PRESS • TAMPA, FLORIDA

Copyright © 2014 by Ira Sukrungruang. All rights reserved.

Cover: "Kannon/Kuan Lin" or "Buddha" street art mural by El Mac and Retna
photographed on the wall of a Los Angeles car wash.
Photograph by Phillip Chardon. Copyright © 2014 by Phillip Chardon.
Back cover photograph by Ruth Wallach, USC Libraries, 2007.
Copyright © 2014 by Ruth Wallach
Reproduced by permission. All rights reserved.

Manufactured in the United States of America
Printed on acid-free paper ∞
First Edition

No part of this book may be reproduced, stored in a retrieval system, or transmitted in
any form or by any means, electronic, mechanical, photocopying, recording, or otherwise,
except as may be expressly permitted by the applicable copyright statutes or in writing by
the publisher.

The University of Tampa Press
401 West Kennedy Boulevard
Tampa, FL 33606

ISBN 978-159732-124-2 (pbk.)
ISBN 978-159732-125-9 (hbk.)

Browse & order online at
www.ut.edu/TampaPress

Library of Congress Cataloging-in-Publication Data

Sukrungruang, Ira.
  Southside Buddhist : essays / Ira Sukrungruang.
    pages cm.
  Includes bibliographical references and index.
  ISBN 978-1-59732-124-2 (pbk : alk. paper) -- ISBN 978-1-59732-125-9 (hbk : alk. paper)
1. Sukrungruang, Ira--Childhood and youth. 2. Thai Americans--Biography. 3. Buddhists--United
States--Biography. 4. Thai Americans--Ethnic identity. 5. Thai Americans--Illinois--Chicago--
Biography. 6. Immigrants--Illinois--Chicago--Biography. 7. Chicago (Ill.)--Biography. I. Title.
  E184.T4S86 2014
  305.8959'11073--dc23   2014030306

for Attila

Table of Contents

I

Be aware the direction the wind blows.

– Thai Proverb

Abridged Immigrant Narrative

Immigrant on the Run

He was quick. Years of running away from mad dogs in Ayutthaya. Years of playing ping-pong with swift-footed monks. Years in the Thai army.

Being small helped. A quarter of the size of the Polish and Irish he worked with, a sliver of their girth. This, however, he would not admit to because he talked big, chest puffed out like a preening rooster.

Roosters are hard to catch, he used to tell his son. When he was young, he chased them along the dusty road, zigzagging and leaping, stumbling and hugging his arms around air and feathers. Finally, he figured out the best way to catch something so erratic was to stay hidden until the last moment.

He used to say that staying alive was about not getting caught. So when the INS chased the illegals through the steel factory in Chicago, he made himself smaller and hid in a locker. Standing and waiting in a locker was no different from outsmarting a rooster. Eventually, he would know when to jump out.

Immigrant Love

It was his mole that attracted her. Some time in 1972.

Since her arrival in America, she rarely had the attention of men, except for the doctors she worked with, who complained about her broken English. She spent her time with her best friend, confiding hopes and dreams, homesickness and fears. What she did not tell her friend was that she yearned for a handsome man to take her out of the crumbling nurses' dorm and into a suburban house where she could raise children. Her younger sister in Thailand was already married and had three kids. She sent photos and letters written on thin blue airmail stationery. At the end of each letter, her sister asked about prospects.

Enter this man with his mole.

She began to feel wanted and needed and desired. And perhaps she had forgotten where she was, forgotten her fears of this country while talking to the man, who was generous with compliments. She did not know he had been married once before. She did not know about the daughter he left in Thailand. She did not know he was in the country illegally. Those details did not matter because he said she had beautiful lips. He said he could read fortunes.

They sat by the fireplace at a party, plates of food on their knees. As she picked at grains of rice, he took out a notebook from his back pocket and drew lines that resembled a tic-tac-toe grid. He started asking her questions: What day were you born? The time? What animal are you in the Chinese Zodiac? After she answered his questions, he smiled. According to this, he said, we will be happy together for a long time.

Immigrant Joy

Immigrants do not experience joy. They are surprised by and suspicious of it. What is this feeling, they wonder, bubbling in their chests? Why does it feel, briefly, comfortable, like home? Why is today not as long as any other day?

Never do they allow themselves to feel, to laugh, to smile, to indulge in the sensation. Never do they let their guard down. They question joy. They think joy comes with false pretenses because, to an immigrant, joy is always short-lived; joy is always closely followed by its opposite.

Immigrant Marriage

Their wedding was not in the familiar heat of Southeast Asia. There were no sisters or brothers or uncles or aunts or cousins. They did not ride on top of an elephant. They did not walk side by side around the temple grounds three times. Their parents did not meet to discuss the compatibility of their union. They did not kneel together in front of monks, heads bent low and praying, while a delicate white string laced through their hands and looped into the palms of a golden statue of Buddha looming above them. They did not partake in the traditional water ceremony where both sides of the family would sprinkle water over the married couple's hands, wishing them luck and a quick baby.

Their wedding took place instead at the Cook County Courthouse. There was a judge. There were a few friends. It was a quick wedding because the line for matrimony was long that day. Behind them was a Hispanic couple. And behind them was an African couple. And behind them a Vietnamese couple and a white couple who did not speak English.

Afterwards, they had a small party at a Chinatown restaurant. A band played a version of Nat King Cole's "Stardust," and though she wanted to dance, he did not. And so she glided by herself, back and forth, pretending to have someone holding her, while he sipped a soda and laughed.

Immigrant Dreams

He took her to open houses in the suburb. Large improbable homes they could never afford. These were houses doctors or lawyers bought. These were houses for immigrants who came to America with money already. Real estate agents tried to push a sale. Imagine, the agents would say, this bedroom as yours. They did imagine themselves occupying this room that was bigger than their apartment in Irving Park. Imagine, the agents would say, your future kids running around in this yard. They did imagine their future kids running around in the yard. They saw a garden, too, with big-fisted dahlias and roses and bitter melons and cucumbers growing along the fence.

He would tell her his dreams of getting rich: the Thai restaurant he wanted to open, the cable company in Thailand he left to a friend to watch over; the fortune telling business, which was getting more clients. He would tell her about how he would be made supervisor at the tile factory and his salary would triple. He would tell her that soon—real soon—they would move out of the apartment into a house of their dreams. He would say America would make this possible. If he were still in Thailand, he would be fixing someone's car. If he were in Thailand, he would be washing someone else's dishes. If he were still in Thailand, he would be drowning.

She did not tell him her dreams. She did not want to interrupt his excitement. She did not want to say these houses scared her because it meant they were moving farther away from her home across the ocean. She did not want to tell him that at night she would wake up and watch him sleep and think he is a wonderful man and she is undeserving of his love. She did not tell him that she listened to the sound Lake Michigan waves and imagined it to be the ocean beckoning her home. She did not tell him that when she dreamed it was always about her father and her brothers and her sisters, and they were calling her back. She did not tell him how glad she was to have found a man like him to dream the appropriate dreams for her because America petrified her.

She clung hard to his hand as they went from room to room, imagining, from house to house, hoping.

Immigrant Son

He was born in 1976 after twenty-four hours of labor and cried for days. The hospital had octagonal windows, and she remembered as she pushed him out, how the rising sun cast a shaft of light on the wall beside her, and it was the light she concentrated on, the light that assuaged her labor pains. Afterwards, the doctor put him in an incubator because he was yellow.

For three days, his mother could not touch him. She watched the rise and fall of his sunken chest. She envied the nurses who came in and out of the room and moved his small arms, listened to his small heart, cleaned his small body. They told her he was getting stronger. They told her she would be able to hold him soon. They told her they never saw a baby born with such thick hair.

His father was in Thailand to check on the cable company that went bankrupt. He called every hour. He asked the same questions.

How is he doing?

Better.

What does he look like?

Small.

What looks like me the most?

His hair.

Over the phone, he laughed loud and proud, and it did not matter that he lost money over a defunct company. He had a son to carry on his name.

When the nurses asked for a name, she thought of her father's. Chua. She thought about how that name would connect her son to the person never far from her heart. She thought of the smoking pipe in his mouth. She thought of his patience. She thought of how it was her father's urging that made her come to America.

In the end, a new life needed a new name. A new name in this new country. She quickly flipped through a book. "Something American," she decided. "Something easy." There is nothing easier than a name with only three letters.

Immigrant Pride

This is my son, he kept saying to anyone who would listen.

Look at him, he said.

Isn't he handsome? he said.

He will be famous, he said.

He will break hearts, he said.

See how black his hair is? he said.

See his birthmark shaped like Thailand? he said.

See how tight he grabs your finger? he said.

He likes to pull my hair, he said.

He makes wonderful noises, he said.

He watches everything, he said.

He watches my every move, he said.

I can't believe he is mine, he kept saying to anyone who would listen.

Immigrant Protection

She held him tight to her. She read that the Hmong kept their infants with them all day, attached to their chests. They never put them down. They were never separated. They slept with them. Ate with them. Bathed with them. This was the reason why Hmong children stuck close to home.

She did not allow anyone to hold him in fear that they would drop him. She held him so tight at times, his young skin bruised. Her friends laughed at her. Said she was creating a mama's boy. Said he would always be stuck to her breast. So be it, she would say.

When her husband was away at work, she spoke to her son.

You love your mama. You love your mama. You love your mama.

She spoke to him in Thai and nothing else. She read Thai books. Told Thai stories. Sang Thai songs. Her favorite song, "Cah Nam Nom," "The Cost of Milk," made her weep every time she sang it, because her milk had gone dry and he was on formula earlier than most. His first word, she told herself, must be in the language she understood.

Immigrant Dreams II

They moved into a house they never thought they could afford. In a suburb. Two floors. White brick. Black roof. They asked a Buddhist monk at the temple in Chicago to come and bless the home. He wore large thick glasses, and because of them, his eyes were magnified like an insect's.

This scared the boy. He cried in his father's arms.

The monk went into every room and sprinkled holy water. He traced a holy symbol with wet white powder on all the doors. He said this house would protect the family from all harm; nothing bad could enter. He said he sensed only good here. He said the boy should sleep in the bedroom that faced east. He said that when the boy slept make sure he didn't face the ceiling. Only bad dreams came to those who slept looking up.

At night, the mother watched her son sleep, watched how he tossed and turned. He was a restless sleeper, one who could end up sideways in the bed. Once, she found him so tangled in his blankets it nearly choked him. This night was no different. When he moved to the flat of his back, his mouth wide open, face toward the ceiling, she gently pushed him onto his side.

There were nights she did not sleep at all, her worry of bad dreams keeping her up. She asked Buddha daily to send only good thoughts when he slept. She asked him for his protection. She asked him why she could not stop worrying, why she felt all of this good fortune would soon disappear.

Immigrant Lessons

When the boy turned five, his father bought him a bike. A real bike. Not a tricycle. Nothing with training wheels. When the father was younger, nearly the same age as his son, his mother threw him into the middle of the river. She told him this was how he was going to learn to swim. If he did not, he would be washed away and drowned. She watched him struggle. She watched him slap at the water. She watched the river take him further away. He said the river made her smaller and smaller. That was the reason he survived. He needed to get to her. He needed to show her how capable he was. And so he swam, clumsily, back to shore. He said his body hurt. He said he coughed out water.

Teaching his son how to ride a bike would be no different. He did not steady the bike. He did not run alongside it. He simply watched the boy get on and fall. Get on and fall. The boy's knees were bloodied. The boy's face was wet.

I don't want to ride anymore, the boy said.

Get on, the father said.

It hurts.

Get on.

The boy got back on and fell. But the time between falls were getting longer now. The boy was learning to pedal. The boy was learning to fall without pain. The boy was no longer crying. Instead, his face was full of determination.

Finally, the boy coasted with ease. It was as if his earlier clumsiness had evaporated.

Look, said the boy. I'm riding.

When the father made it to shore those many years ago, after he had coughed out the river's water, he looked up for his mother, but she had gone home without word or praise.

I'm very proud, said the father. You ride well.

Immigrant Borders

The immigrant comes in search of a larger world, only to find a smaller one. Yes, the land is expansive. Yes, it stretches across deserts and mountains and prairies. But the immigrant only feels safe, feels free, in the space of home. There are invisible borders here. Around the house to the front of the driveway. Inside this space, the immigrant can do what he or she pleases. The immigrant can cook stinky food. The immigrant can pray in any language, to anyone. The immigrant can say aloud, "America is a peculiar place." The immigrant can raise a son any way he or she wishes.

Within these borders, the son is Thai, not American.

Once, on a hot summer day, the son rode his bike up and

down the driveway. The father was at work at the tile factory. The mother sewed inside, watching him from the front window. He did endless loops. He loved the sensation of wind whizzing in his ears. His lobes were long. His mother told him they were like Buddha's, and when he went fast, they fluttered. He knew the border. He knew he could not ride past the driveway and into the street. He had heard this lecture countless times. He was at the age, however, of testing boundaries. He wanted to know how fast he could go. He wanted to know how fast he could make his earlobes flutter.

So he pedaled. Hard. His muscle pulsed. Hard. He breathed. Hard. The end of the driveway came and went and he was on the blacktop of the street, his ears fluttering like a speed bag. Wind whooshed.

His exhilaration was short lived.

A car blared on its horn. Swerved. Missed. Sped away. Shouted "Fuck" out the open window.

The mother stormed out of the house. She yanked him by one earlobe. She threw him down on the grass. She hit his legs, his arms, his back, any unprotected part of him. It did not matter that the neighbors were out. It did not matter that other children saw this small Thai woman, this small immigrant woman, hitting her son repeatedly. She was blind to their gazes.

How many times? she said. How many times do I tell you?

The boy cried. Grass blades poked his face. He promised not to do it again, but he knew this to be a lie. He would do it again. He would pedal even faster next time. He liked the feeling of speed; he liked the sound; he liked the danger. He marveled at the word "fuck."

The borders expanded.

The mother knew this, which was why she hit harder, which was why she kept saying to him, Listen to your mother, and don't do that again, and I can't lose you. It was why she picked him up and held him hard to her chest, held him so hard he said he could not breathe.

Immigrant Loyalty

Question: What is the best country in the world?
Answer: Thailand.
Question: Who is the greatest man in the world?
Answer: Daddy.
Question: And?
Answer: The King.
Question: Who else?
Answer: Buddha.
Question: What language should you speak all the time?
Answer: Thai.
Question: What are you?
Answer: I am Thai.

Immigrant Dream III

In the summer, he mowed the lawn. In the fall, he raked the leaves. In the winter, he shoveled the snow.

In the summer, she took care of their son. In the fall, she took care of their son. In the winter, she took care of their son.

Both were content. Both had fulfilled a shared dream.

When one dream is achieved, what do we do? Do we stop dreaming?

An Immigrant's Dream is not an American one. An American Dream revolves around one notion: Success. An Immigrant's Dream revolves around one notion: Survival.

Now the two of them began to dream for their son. The father wanted a professional golfer. The mother wanted a doctor. The father wanted to continue living in the States. The mother wanted her son to marry someone Thai and eventually return to his ancestral home.

The boy. He dreamed of being a boy.

Immigrant Fear

The boy stood next to his mother at the bank. He could barely see over the counter. He eyed the candy dish. He was six and wanted nothing to do with this; somewhere in his young brain, he knew this would be his role for the rest of his life.

The bank teller asked, Can I help you?

The boy stared up at his mother and then at the bank teller. He said, My mother would like to deposit some money into her account.

The bank teller looked down at the boy, smiled, and then at the woman beside him. She asked the woman, What is your account number?

The mother spoke to the boy and the boy translated. He handed the bank teller a check.

The bank teller said, This check won't clear right away.

The mother told the boy to ask the woman why.

The amount is large, said the bank teller. It will take a couple of days.

The mother frowned. She spoke to the boy again.

The boy rolled his eyes. The mother nudged him. The boy sighed. The mother cleared her throat. The boy looked at the bank teller, as if to say he was sorry for all of this. He then said, My mother would like to know the exact date the check will clear. She would also like to have your name and number, so she can contact you if the check does not get into the account. She would also like to add that last month's statement came late in the mail and would like to make sure that would not happen again.

After everything was settled, the boy asked the bank teller for a green lollipop, his favorite.

The boy found himself talking to accountants and waitresses and sales clerks. He inquired about bra sizes and ordered whenever his parents went to an American restaurant.

When the boy got older, he asked the mother why she could not talk for herself. He knew she could speak English. Speak it relatively well.

She was older, gray creeping into her thinning hair. She said

American people were like that one monster villain the boy was so afraid of.

Freddy Kruger?

The mother nodded. American people were like Freddy Kruger. They stole her voice.

Immigrant Fear II

The man never let negative thinking enter his brain. He did not want to admit that he was sixty and none of his plans were coming to fruition and he had been working at the same factory for years, the same factory that scarred his hands, and he was not a rich gas station owner and he did not have a restaurant. He did not want to admit that the woman he loved, still loved, did not love him as much as she loved their son. Not even close. He did not remember the last kind thing she said to him. He did not remember that last time they were intimate. He did not want to admit that on some days he did not want to come home, but rather, he wanted to drive all night through the lighted city. He did not want to admit that women at the temple still found him attractive, even though that mole had hair on it. He did not want to admit that he found them attractive too. He did not want to admit the guilt he sometimes thought about feeling, about how he left his other family in Thailand, about how he did not treat his son well on the golf course, about how he sometimes pushed a little too hard for his own gain, about how he talked big but it was always just talk.

To admit all of this was to admit his unhappiness. He was not unhappy. He loved America. He repeated this.

I love America. I love America. I love America.

Immigrant Fear III

When the boy turned thirteen, he began making and receiving phone calls. To and from white girls. The mother sometimes picked up the phone. She would say in bad English, Who is calling?

The girls on the other end of the line would tell her their names.

It's Jean. It's Claudia. It's Brenna. It's Heidi. It's Jenny. It's April. It's Sara. It's Dalphine. It's Vicky.

She would sigh and hand the phone over to her son, and he would talk for an hour or so before hanging up.

Once, the mother quietly picked up the phone to eavesdrop on her son's conversations with these white girls. She anticipated gossip about school. She anticipated innocent chatter.

She heard: Will you be my butt doctor?

She heard her son: I have advance degrees in being a butt doctor.

She heard: My butt is in need of doctoring.

She heard her son: Let's make an appoint to fix your butt.

The mother hung up. Panic stabbed at her chest; it felt like a hundred sharp syringes into the heart.

Immigrant Regret

Throughout the course of an immigrant's life, regret is never far behind. The immigrant has feelings of regret daily, hourly, by the minute or second. Buddha teaches that regret and guilt are the worst forms of suffering because they cannot be easily erased. They follow. They linger.

The man regretted stealing his friend's student visa all those years ago. The woman regretted leaving her family behind. Coming to America, for an immigrant, is a form of regret.

For most of their lives together, they tried to look beyond their regret and guilt. What was there to regret, they wondered, when we live in a beautiful home, in a good neighborhood, with two cars, and a son who can do no wrong? Why feel guilty, they wondered, when there is so much to celebrate?

Like their son winning golf tournaments. Like their son doing reasonably well in school. Like their son receiving the American Legion Award on graduation day. He stood on stage, in blue robes, with a plaque cradled in his arms. He was asked to make a speech. The parents waited for him to say how much he loved them. They waited for him to say that they had made many sacrifices for the betterment of his life.

Instead, he said: It's good to be an American.

He walked off the stage to roars. The parents clapped, too; they did not know what else to do.

The Immigrant Son . . .

. . . is no longer a boy. He is now in his thirties, married to a *farang*, white foreigner, and lives in Florida, a state whose climate is near to his ancestral land. Hot and muggy. His parents have moved back to Thailand. They are divorced. He talks to his mother once a week. He talks to his father occasionally. The son goes to temple once a month, for the food, not for Buddha. He says prayers to himself, all those prayers that his parents made him remember and recite every night.

Sometimes a friend will ask about his family. Where are they living now?

In Thailand, he says.

Do you have family here in the states?

Just my wife's.

Any Thai family?

No.

Is it lonely?

The immigrant son shrugs. Says, Not really.

The truth: An immigrant is always lonely, and an immigrant son will inherit that loneliness. He will recognize the loneliness at odd moments. Driving to work, and he will remember how his father drove to the tile factory every day, and how he must have stared beyond the road in front of him, a road perhaps that would have led to a life where all his dreams came true. Looking out the window of his Florida home and the immigrant son will remember his mother sitting by their front window in the Chicago suburb, filling her days by sewing, her hands working on outfit after outfit, day by day, the sun rising and falling.

He knows that his immigrant parents came with expectations. He knows they had expectations for him. He wonders, at times, whether he has let them down. He wonders whether this loneliness will ever go away and suddenly he will truly know what it means to be of one country but to live in another. The immigrant son understands that this tug and pull will be there his entire life. The immigrant son understands that he is trying to live two lives at once: the one his parents sought for him, and the one he sought for himself. The immigrant son understands that when his wife talks about home it is easy for her to identify, and when he thinks about home he thinks of not a place but of immigrants.

The immigrant son understands.

Tots-R-Us

There were two ways we could get there. One: take South-west Highway to Cicero and then Cicero to Archer. This was the simplest route. When we passed Midway Airport, I knew we were almost there. Planes sometimes roared above the Beetle and I put my hands over my ears, the earth shaking underneath me. Sometimes a plane taxied down the runway, and I asked my father where it came from. On bad days, he kept his hand on the steering wheel, his eyes on the road. On good days, he said, "Thailand."

"How far is Thailand?"

"Very," he said. He took his hands off the wheel and spread them wide apart, as if that space were filled with oceans and mountains and prairies. He said Thailand was so far that as the sun rose here, it set there. Thailand was so far that roosters spoke a different language. My father looked at my mother in the back seat. "Am I right?"

She smiled and tugged lightly at my hair. "Thailand is so far," she said in Thai, "that once you make it there you never want to come back."

And my parents began to laugh, and I laughed with them even though I didn't know why.

Good days: Laughter and talk of Thailand.

Bad days: Quiet and FM 100 elevator music.

Two: take smaller streets because we had extra time. My father cruised around the neighborhood. I knew the houses. The one with the gnomes in the front yard. One with a black lawn jockey holding a lantern. One with a yappy Jack Russell, which I sometimes rolled the window down to bark back at. I knew the name of the streets, and my mother and I sang them out loud, block by block.

"Luna! Linder! Lotus! Long! Lorel!"

I wanted my father to continue driving. "Further," I said.

"Further." Never pull over to let me out at Tots-R-Us Daycare and Preschool. Drive and drive and drive, following the sun until it began to rise again in some distant land that wasn't Chicago. And when the rooster cleared its throat and sang a new song, I would know we were in another world.

꘍

But I was already in another world. There were two worlds I was trying to make sense of, the one I was suddenly thrust in and the one in my head. In one world, I had beans and franks for lunch, and in the other one, I ate pink and turquoise globs of the fantastic. Both tasted good. Both were filling.

One night before I started attending Tots-R-Us, I remember watching an episode of *20/20* with my mother. News shows were boring, but *20/20* was a Thursday night routine. One of the show's segments was about Toys-R-Us, a mega toy store. On trips to Toys-R-Us, I barricaded myself with stuffed animals, lost in a world of plush. After watching *20/20*, however, I never wanted to step foot in Toys-R-Us again.

Toys-R-Us was haunted. A night security man stated that toys moved on their own. While closing up the store, a worker thought she heard whispering among the GI Joe men. There were other odd occurrences: Barbie dolls blinked. R/C cars revved up their engines without batteries. It took very little to get my brain going. In my other world, possessed toys chased after me with brightly colored weapons. In my other world, Darth Vader and Raggedy Ann and Andy interrogated me about the empty bag of shrimp chips. A week after watching the *20/20* episode, my mother and I drove by a Toys-R-Us on Cicero. A shopping cart raced across an empty parking lot and smashed into a light pole.

When my mother and father dropped me off at Tots-R-Us for the first time, I had it in my head I was going to a haunted Toys-R-Us. It was six thirty, winter, and the sun wasn't up yet. Archer Avenue was dark. The window display of Tots-R-Us had porcelain dolls in various poses that reminded me of the images on TV. I cried as my mother tried to ease me out of the car. I don't remember how she eventually got me out, but this I will never forget.

I ripped my hand from her grip and took off running. I ran down the block. I ran as hard as I could. I liked the sensation of my legs and arms pumping, liked the sensation of speed and the sound of it in my ears. I could easily get away, I remember thinking, if I just kept running, kept moving fast. For a second, I had forgotten that I was afraid of the haunted Tots-R-Us. For a second, I thought if I could keep running nothing in the world would ever get me. I spotted a U.S. mailbox at the end of the block, and beyond that the sky had begun to lighten, and beyond that the clouds were wispy. I aimed for the sky and felt I could reach it, lift off and into the blue. But a hand grabbed mine and yanked me to an abrupt stop. Yanked me right into cradling arms and a heaving chest. I could feel a heartbeat out of sync with mine. I could hear a voice, but did not know whose it was or what it was saying. I was still in the sky.

When I came to, I was in Tots-R-Us and a woman was taking me away from my mother, a woman who had short-cropped hair, who was asking me in a sing-song voice, "What's your name? What's your name, my little man?"

❧

"My name is Dawn." She had rosy cheeks. She had a sweet voice. "What's your name?"

I put a red block on top of a green block. I was building a Christmas wall.

"His name is Ira," my friend Chico said. "My name is Chico."

She furrowed her brow. "I didn't ask *you*."

Chico didn't seem deterred by Dawn. He smiled at her like he had not heard a word she said. Chico's dimples could eat your fingers. "Would you like to build a wall with us?" he asked.

"Nooooo," said Dawn. "I want to be married." She looked at me and smiled. I put another block on top of another. "Do you want to marry me, Ira?"

I shrugged. I didn't know what marry meant.

"I'll marry you," said Chico. "My cousin said you have lots of fun when you get married."

Dawn shook her head. She put a Cracker Jack ring in my hand. "All you have to do is give me this ring and say I do. Can you do that?"

I nodded.

I put the ring in her hand and told her I do.

"I do, too," she said. "Now we're married."

"You gotta have a baby now," said Chico. "My cousin said once you get married the babies keep coming."

Dawn pulled me to a toy basket. "He's right. We need a baby." The basket was filled with trucks and bears and jump ropes and balls. She reached in and pulled out a blonde baby doll. "Here's our baby, Ira." The doll had blue eyes. It had pigtails. Its skin was the color of a light peach. "Let's call her Mindy."

I nodded. I liked the TV show *Mork and Mindy*.

Throughout that morning, we walked the baby. We fed the baby imaginary bananas. We sang to the baby. We burped the baby. We changed the baby. Chico followed us and chimed in here and there. "Can I hold the baby?" "The baby is hungry." "The baby wants to play with Uncle Chico." Dawn ignored him and hummed and did domestic things like folding pieces of clothing or pretending to cook meals.

About an hour into being married, Dawn said, "You have to go to work." She said that if I didn't work then we'd have no money and if we didn't have any money then we would live on the streets and if we lived on the streets Mindy would die from the cold.

"Where do I work?" I said.

"At the fire department with me," said Chico.

Once a fireman came to Tots-R-Us and talked about how we shouldn't play with matches. He told us if we ever caught on fire we should stop, drop, and roll. Then he put on music and we stopped, dropped, and rolled.

"Do whatever you want," said Dawn. "But go to work." Chico and I started on our way to the Fire Department. It was at the other end of the daycare. Halfway there, Dawn ran to me and took my hand, pulling me under a plastic table. We sat in the shadow of the tablecloth.

"You forgot to give me a good-bye kiss."

I stared at her.

"Do this." Dawn puckered her lips.

I puckered mine.

She moved in and our lips connected. It was wet and warm. I pulled away and wiped my mouth.

"Go to work now," she said, smiling. "I'll have dinner ready."

When I crawled from under the table, Chico was jumping up and down, pointing at the other end of the room. "We gotta get going," he said. "Look." I followed his finger. The flames, the smoke. I had to go to work. Save lives. Tell people to stop, drop, and roll. When I looked back at Dawn one last time before saving the world, she held Mindy in the air, saying what a beautiful baby she was, Daddy was coming home soon, and weren't we the perfect happy family?

౭౨

Yes we were.

Our happiness existed inside that car traveling along Chicago streets, making its way to daycare. Bad days or not, there was safety in the Volkswagen Beetle, and safety was the closest thing to happiness for my immigrant parents. Outside the car was the unknown. Dangers lurked in the guise of language and culture. My parents were out of sync with the rhythms of this land, a city where skyscrapers jutted from concrete foundations.

Where were the dusty dogs? Where was the hot sun that steamed dirt roads? Where were the yawning fields of rice, the ox that pulled the plow, the croaking geckos?

I had been to Thailand only once then, and seen the home my parents spoke of. In that visit, I felt something I could not name. Not then. Not at three. Or four. Or twenty-nine. Suddenly, the world was not full of afternoon naps on white cots and lunch where the cook made mashed potatoes from a box of flakes. I no longer colored in coloring books because Thailand *was* a coloring book. Green moved in snaky tendrils and red was like a breathless slap.

When we returned to Chicago, I blinked for days afterwards.

"What's wrong with your eyes?" Chico said.

I told him the light was wrong.

I blinked. I blinked.

"What are you saying?"

The light, I told him. The light.

Chico tilted his curly head. One collar of his shirt was up, one was down. He backed away, and then he turned and ran.

When my mother came to pick me up, a woman with a mole on her left cheek took my mother and me aside and said: "Your son's acting very strange."

I blinked. I blinked.

"Like that," the woman said. "Look at him."

My mother blinked, too. Blinked twice more before she flicked my forehead.

I stopped.

"And he's been speaking gibberish," the woman said. "He's been scaring the other kids. Poor Chico hid in the corner all day." She pointed into the daycare and Chico rolled around against the back wall. He kept looking my way.

My mother asked me what was going on.

I told her I wanted an elephant. A white elephant.

"You see? What's he saying?"

My mother flicked my head again. Talk English, she told me.

"I want an elephant. A white elephant."

The woman smiled. "He's fixed."

My mother nodded.

I waved to Chico and said, "Good-bye," and he waved back and said, "Good-bye." For him, the world had righted itself, and his friend had come back from whatever place he had been.

Outside sat the Beetle. The door was open. I could hear Mary Chapin Carpenter singing on the radio. I could see my father tapping his fingers on the steering wheel. I rushed into the car.

ళ

There was no rush getting to the park that day. The new teacher believed in taking her time. Her favorite word was "easy," as in "Take it easy now," or "Easy there, youngsters," or "That's so easy." Her hair fell to mid-back and she liked to tangle her fingers in it. She wasn't like the other teachers. She wore bright colors with swirls in them and rose-colored sunglasses. She was a lot younger than the other teachers, whose faces were like cracked earth.

That afternoon we journeyed to a different park. Usually, we went to a municipal one with a rocket slide and cargo net. That one was 204 steps away. The new teacher led us to another park, hidden in a neighborhood. I held her hand, Chico held the other, and she hummed a song I didn't know. When we got to the park I told Chico it was 509 steps. He smiled. The rest of the kids were working on counting to ten, but I had been counting since I was two, counting in Thai and in English.

The park was empty. Dandelions sprouted everywhere and I wanted to pick them all and give them to the new teacher. Instead, Chico and I went straight for the sandbox. The other kids fought for swings and rocking horses. The teacher found a bench and said, "Take it easy now, kiddies." Her sunglasses hid her eyes.

Chico was building a little metropolis. He made a teepee in the sand and called it the Sears Tower. He made another one and said it was the Sears Tower 2. I traced a stick in the sand, chasing army ants and making wavy designs.

Not long after we arrived, two kids from the house across the street came into the park. They had crew cuts. They looked like twins except one wore a black T-shirt and the other a green one. Their bare feet slapped against the concrete. They headed straight for the sandbox.

The one in the black shirt stomped across Chico's city. Chico looked up, but didn't say anything. These boys were about the same age as us, but they were bigger than Chico.

"This is our sandbox," the boy in green said. "Leave." He pushed me over. My ear went into the sand.

"Easy there," the new teacher said. She didn't move from the bench, but began wagging her finger. The sight of her there, calm and cool, put me at ease, despite the sand in my ear.

The two boys glared at the teacher and spit. Then they darted across the street, back to the house. It didn't take long for them to come back with their older sister. She led the way, her dark hair flowing behind her. She pointed at the teacher, at us, saying rapid words I didn't understand.

The teacher rose and put her hands up. "Easy," she said.

"Don't you raise your hands at me, bitch," the girl said. She was plump. Her finger looked like a pale sausage.

The two boys stood on either side of Chico and started kicking sand at him. He put his arm up and turned his face the other way.

"Easy," said the teacher. "We don't want any trouble."

"You got trouble now, chica." The girl moved to within an inch of my teacher's face. I thought they were going to kiss. By then, I was an expert at kissing.

"All right, time to go," the teacher said. She backed away. She called out to the other kids who had stopped what they were doing to watch.

"That's right," said the girl. "You get these brats out of our park."

"Easy," said the teacher and this time, her voice was no longer the soothing lilt like when she read from those picture books. It was deep and she stared right at the girl and held her gaze. "We're leaving."

The girl backed away and said, "You got two minutes. If you're still here with these brats we gonna teach you never to come back." She turned and said something to the boys. They followed her.

When they were gone, Chico rose from the sand and brushed himself off. He looked down at the ground so no one would see he was crying.

The teacher knelt down in front of him. She patted his curls and blew sand off his cheeks. "We're all OK," she said and began to lead everyone out, humming again.

As soon as we stepped out of the park, the boys across the street began screaming like an alarm. They brought a bucket of apples and launched them at us. The new teacher yelled at them to stop, but apples were landing on the concrete, splattering at our feet. We didn't have a choice. We ran.

I was the biggest. I was the slowest.

An apple hit me smack on the side of my head. I felt my heart start to beat where the apple hit. I saw Chico far ahead of me. I saw everyone far ahead of me. Chico turned as he ran. He mouthed something I didn't hear. I didn't hear anything but my heart. It was so loud. One of the boys ran after me. He caught up. He screamed, his mouth like a cave, but all I could hear was my heart. He took out an orange thumbtack and pushed it into my arm. I saw his laughter. His wide mouth opening and closing, his yellow teeth like a saw. I didn't feel the tack. I didn't feel anything but the pavement on my feet, the thumping on the side of my head. I couldn't run fast enough. I couldn't catch up. They were so far ahead. Everyone, Chico, everyone.

I stopped.

The boys laughed behind me. I grabbed the side of my

head. It was swollen. I thought the apple was stuck in it. I didn't scream. I didn't cry. I remembered my mother always telling me to never cry in public, never show any weakness. The teacher and the other kids waited at the end of the block. They waved for me to hurry. Chico stared at the ground again, his chin plastered to his chest.

When I reached them, the teacher said, "Oh, honey," and she took the tack out of my arm and held me tight. I nestled into her, wanting the day to end like that.

Back at Tots-R-Us, I sat at a lunch table the rest of the afternoon with ice on my head and a band-aid on my arm. I thought about the boys and the park that was 509 steps away. Chico sat beside me, but we didn't say much. We were both sorting out what had happened as well as five-year-olds could. Me, I remembered my heart. I remembered my legs and their limitations. You can't run forever, I learned. Your heart might explode, I learned. Not all sandboxes are mine, I learned. There were other lessons, ones I couldn't understand until much later, ones I'm still sorting out even now.

But that day, Chico knew where he stood in the world. You could see that in his puckered face, his wet eyes, his silence. There was understanding I couldn't fathom.

At the end of the day, my mother asked what had happened and the teacher told her we ran into some trouble at the park. Nothing too bad. It was easily handled.

৵৹

It wasn't easy, the song we were to sing when we graduated from Tots-R-Us. The weeks before the nighttime graduation ceremony, we practiced singing and moving in sync. Chico believed the louder he was the better he sounded and Dawn just moved her lips but nothing came out. For a finale, the teachers at Tots-R-Us thought that Dawn and I should dance. I wasn't the best colorer or quickest reader. I didn't know my left from my right yet. But for the last two years at Tots-R-Us, Dawn and I were the best dancers.

Tots-R-Us was transformed into a disco club. Streamers hung all over the room. There was a disco ball over the stage where the toy chests were usually kept. Our last art projects were taped to the walls. I wore a brown suit that day. Chico a white one. Dawn floated in a light blue dress and a tiara. We lined up in front of our parents. Fathers snapped pictures. Mothers clapped before the music even started. When the record played, the graduating preschool class of Tots-R-Us began to sing: *The sun'll come out tomorrow. Bet your bottom dollar that tomorrow, there'll be sun!*

We swayed back and forth. Chico kept bumping into my shoulder, swaying in the wrong direction. Dawn held my hand.

Just thinkin' about tomorrow clears away the cobwebs and the sorrow 'til there's none!

My mother and father sat close together, next to Chico's mother, who clutched her hands in front of her like in prayer. When we finished, our parents rose and clapped, and the boys bowed and the girls curtsied.

Then it was the dance. Dawn and I stood in the middle of the floor. The lights dimmed and the disco ball spun, reflecting tiny lights around the room. *I Saw Her Standing There* by the Beatles blared out from the record player, and I took Dawn into my arms and we went with the music. Nobody taught us any of this. It looked good, felt good. As she spun, her tiara shining like a constellation, I didn't know this was the last day I would see her, the last time I would dance or kiss any girl again until I was twelve. I didn't know this was the last time I would see Chico, who was snapping his fingers in beat with the drums. A few months later, I would turn six and a few after that I would be going to another school only two blocks from home and there would be harder things to learn, harder things to overcome. But Dawn and I danced, and Chico snapped, and John Lennon and Paul McCartney sang.

There are always two ways of getting somewhere. Sometimes there are more.

Playing with Buddha

I was always taken by the figure of the meditating Buddha in our living room in Chicago: his straight-backed posture, his wide shoulders and narrow waist, his elegant hands resting humbly on his lap. When I was young, I used to stare at him for long minutes. He sat in the family room, on a shelf seven feet high. Around him were other Buddhas, two yellow candles, and a cup of rice to stabilize incense. This statue could rest comfortably in my palm and weighed no more than a couple of pounds. Yet he was heavy in spiritual weight, my father always said; the weight that seeped into our family, that made us believe we could go another day in this country, that made us believe.

The Buddha was not native to America. He had been in my father's family for years, ever since he was a barefoot boy running wildly in the late 1930s in Ayutthaya, Thailand. I wondered if he, too, felt misplaced in this new world, a world so different from the heat and humidity of his native home, a world without the familiar sounds of geckos and the shrill calls of mynahs and the evening song of croaking frogs. This was America. This was Illinois. This was Chicago. Here, the house shook on Mondays when the garbage truck rumbled by. Here, our neighbor Jack rode endless loops on his riding lawn mower. Here, mosquitos sucked a different type of nectar.

My family revolved around this Buddha. Each morning, before I went off to school, I prayed to him. Some days, my mother allowed me to use a dining room chair to stand on and deliver a shot glass of coffee—cream, no sugar. Some days she let me light the candles and incense before we prayed in the evenings. I was supposed to close my eyes and think only good thoughts. My eyes remained open, however, fixed on him. I imagined, at any moment, he would rise and float down like an autumn leaf. I imagined he would impart vital secrets, and I could ask him the questions that had long plagued me. And there, in the living room, he would walk onto the palms of my hands and we would spend the evening—boy and Buddha—speaking like friends.

෴

Friends. During the time when I had few, Buddha became the closest thing to amity. I don't remember how it happened, but the Buddha in the living room took on more meaning than just an icon of worship. "He is with you," my mother used to say. "Believe in him."

And so I believed that he was more than a bronze statue, that he was solid like a body is solid, the way it gives a bit when you lean against it, the way it molds to accept the presence of another. He possessed the gift of language and was bilingual like me, skipping freely between English and Thai. We spoke often, our conversations in hushed whispers, and he sounded soothing, not harsh like my elementary school principal or gargled like the monks at temple. Buddha was the holder of my secrets. He understood that loneliness and emptiness were one and the same. At the age of seven, I was lonely and empty. Though I did not know it, I felt it, like ripples in water.

I felt other things, too. I felt too much. That was my problem. I was a child who suffered from a serious dose of shyness, and that shyness made my heart quicken when someone spoke to me, made me feel ill-at-ease in unfamiliar places, made my body quiver and shake, my every sense on edge until I either cried uncontrollably, or worse, shut down.

This happened often; so often my second grade teacher asked my mother to come for a meeting one afternoon.

Mrs. Slusarchak was a patient teacher, who lived in Munster, Indiana. "I live in Munster," she said, "like the stinky cheese." I always thought she said Monster, and imagined hairy demons, living in cheese-shaped houses. I liked her. She wore bright dresses—Hawaiian pastels—that seemed to ward off the dreary Chicago winter days. She looked pretty with her short hair and small glasses and laughed with her whole body.

My mother came straight from work that afternoon, still in her nurse's uniform. She smiled timidly and sat across from Mrs. S, her purse on her lap. I was next to her, aiming my eyes out the window at the swing set I didn't get on during recess because Tommy W wouldn't let me.

Mrs. S told my mother I wasn't in trouble. She said I was a darling of a student, a math champ every week, and my penmanship was the best in the class. My mother patted my head and said, "We practice everyday."

"I can tell," Mrs. S said and let out a laugh that nearly knocked my mother off the chair. When she calmed, she said, "But I'm concerned about his behavior."

"Has he been bad?" my mother said.

Mrs. S shook her head. "Not in the least. He's just terribly shy."

She went on to talk about what happened at recess. How I wanted to get on the swing but Tommy W told me to go away, so I did and sat on the bench, staring at my hands. This was what I did often, she said. Stare at my hands. I could never meet her eyes. I could never speak more than two words at a time. "There are days," she said, "I would not hear a word from him."

"Is this true?" my mother asked me in Thai.

I stared at my hands. My mother sighed. It was a sigh that said she knew exactly what Mrs. S was talking about. It was a sigh that said she, too, was like this—this fear that gripped our being and wouldn't relent, this fear that made her hide in her room reading magazines or made her sew endless dresses she would never wear. This fear that danger could come from any direction, so the less noticed we became the safer we were.

"I'm sorry for him," my mother said. "He is like me."

Mrs. S nodded. She understood. She suggested my mother enroll me in Cub Scouts or other activities, so I could be around other people, so I would be forced to interact in a social setting, so I might meet friends. My mother agreed, and the next day, she sent me to school with a bagful of apples for my teacher.

What I wanted to say was I had a friend: Buddha. Within him was a heart that beat strong, that pulsated to the core of the earth, that awakened something in me.

This was not a spiritual awakening, not a recognition beyond the self as many theologians would define it. Nor was it a sudden epiphany to a transcendent crisis. I was too young to comprehend such lofty ideas, too young to fully understand what Buddhism was or why my family was so devoted to it. I was awakened in the way a newborn registers it has fingers and toes, and those fingers and toes have function; in the way you realize that if you see one bird, you might see another and another, that you are not as alone as you thought you were, that the world is filled with birds, or in this case, with Buddhas, and every Buddha is a friend.

I don't know how it happened, but one day I began talking to him in the living room. The contents of our conversation have dug into the recesses of my brain, but I do remember my mother asking from the kitchen who I was speaking to.

"Buddha," I said.

"Excellent," she said. "Speak to him every day, OK?"

༄

"I spoke to him every day," my friend said. "His name was Bob." My friend and I were in our early twenties, and the best place to be on a hot summer evening in Chicago was an over-air-conditioned bar. He was relaying tales of his imaginary friend during a time when he lived clear across the ocean, growing up in a semi-affluent family in Poland.

"What did you two talk about?" I asked.

"Bob was well-versed in all subjects."

We laughed, making light of the conversation, as if we couldn't believe how naïve we once were.

"Do you remember when he started appearing?" I said.

"About the time when my mom was about to ditch my dad and come here."

"You think that's why Bob appeared?"

My friend shrugged and seemed to speak more to his drink than to me. "I remember what he looked like though."

He went on to describe Bob, who had crazy wild hair that went in all directions. Bob, who always appeared in a blue and white striped sweater and khaki shorts. Bob, who was always barefoot.

"Isn't that crazy?" he said.

It wasn't crazy. I shook my head.

"What's crazier," my friend said, "is I thought I saw him the other day. At work."

"An older Bob or young Bob?

"The same Bob."

"Was he barefoot?" I asked.

"Can't be barefoot in Home Depot. But he had on the same sweater and he was holding hands with his dad, I guess."

I have been reading articles about seeing flashes of people from our other lives. My friend and Bob might have been something in another incarnation. These old acquaintances come in flashes or take on the form of an imaginary friend when young. Once we become older our minds try hard to make sense of this but can't. One of my friends—a wiccan— says it is like we are taken to the edge of understanding and beyond that is a black void. What exist are flashes. Glimpses. What follows is a strong sense of loss.

"Are you sure it was Bob?" I asked.

"Nope." My friend ordered another drink. "When you talk about imaginary friends you really can't be sure of anything."

∽

I can't be sure of my friend Buddha either. But I can be sure that when I was six I was picked on, I was bullied. I am sure that I was born an only child and occupied much of my time by myself. I am sure that I am the son of two immigrant parents, who loved me with all their being, even more than they loved each other, and sometimes, because of this love, they smothered me with suffocating affection. I am sure that my family was scared and they, too, turned to Buddha for day-to-day guidance through this world that was not Thailand, that snowed when there should be hot devouring sun. I am sure that I possessed an over-active imagination. I am sure that when I felt overwhelmed I hid myself within the darkness of my arms, made the world sound hollow like a cave. I am sure that the safest place in the world when I was small was the back of my mother's knees. I am sure that the mind is a mysterious muscle, and the mind of a child is even more mysterious.

And of this I am positive: every time I looked at the Buddha in the living room, I found myself calm, serene, as if caught in a moment before waking or sleeping.

☙

Before I went to sleep, I talked to Buddha. My parents were trying to reclaim their bedroom. Up until then, I wedged myself between them on my father's homemade bed. I was a husky boy and prone to tossing and turning. When I was three or four, this was fine, but now I possessed a larger body that took up more of the bed, and my father was tired of having my hand slapping his face.

My new room scared me, even though my mother and father painted it the light shade of blue I asked for, even though I had been in it countless times in the daylight. Darkness changed the landscape of the room. No longer did the sun filter through the blinds. In the dark, there was an absence of color, and that absence felt oppressive. The room was empty save for a twin bed and a metal desk. There was barely anything on the walls, except for a small Buddha pendant hanging above the bed and a picture of my father when he was a monk. The room seemed too big, sonorous, though it was only half the size of my parents'. I felt there were places for monsters to hide, especially the cavernous closet. If the closet door was open, when I peered into the black space of its cavity, I convinced myself there were things that existed in there. Unpleasant things.

The first few weeks, I ended up back in my parents' bed until my father put his foot down. "Big boys sleep in their own rooms," he said. "You are a big boy, yes?"

I nodded.

"Nothing can hurt you," he said. "Buddha protects us."

I needed Buddha to be more than a presence, more than a statue, and so I made him real. He sat crossed legged on my bed, not in a meditating fashion, but how I sat when Mrs. S read to us. My Buddha did not speak sage advice. He adopted schoolyard lingo, and told me the kids at school were dork noses and I was so much better than they were. At night, Buddha eased me to sleep with his wild stories. "One time," he'd begin and the tale would take off in bizarre and outrageous directions, always ending with a hero who stood tall and was not afraid to take on the world. We played rock, paper, scissors, and he was always shocked when I beat him. But when the darkest part of the night came, he hovered above me, and I could feel the heat of his presence. His skin glowed, a night-light.

೧

It's like a light switch. One day they are there and the next they are not. This is true of real friends, also. The friends we have when we are in school. What happens to them? Jody is now a photographer in North Carolina. Casey works for USAA in Texas. Andrea is a schoolteacher in Illinois. What we share is a past, a period in time. We become a memory. We become part of a sentence that begins with, "Remember Ira . . ."

But seldom do we remember our imagined friends, because to admit to this is somehow to admit to a deficiency on our part. Yet they existed, too. They were essential, especially in those formative years, those years perhaps when we needed a friend to listen to our every problem, to tell us we were never alone.

But perhaps, we want to keep our friends a secret. To protect them from ridicule, from sideway glances. They protected us when we were younger, and now, it's our turn to protect them.

"Remember Buddha," I want to say. "Dude told the craziest stories."

☙

There are other stories. Once I watched over a boy who had an imaginary friend. I was twenty, and the boy was about five. He was quiet, but exuberant whenever I asked him about his favorite cartoon, *Teen Titans*. The curious thing about our conversation was that he always referred to himself in the "we." When I asked him about it, he said he and his friend watched the cartoon every day. Then he turned to an empty chair and smiled.

"It's a phase," his mother said. "I had one myself."

Many have.

Dr. Lawrence Kutner, better known as Dr. Dad, says imaginary friends are common in childhood and that children create them to try to understand an adult world.

I did not understand the adult world; I only reacted to it. Faced with adversity I shut down. I let my brain take me to a safe place in my head, the one I created to shelter me from whatever worries chased me. In that shelter I was never alone.

"I'm here," Buddha would say.

And we played in lotus-filled ponds. And the sun always brought rainbows. And the world was without darkness. In the classroom, he made himself small and sat on my shoulder. He whispered in my ear. *Look at Eric. He's sooooo fat. Danny is the stinkiest. Tommy's a fart head.* Sometimes I giggled out loud and drew the attention of my classmates. Sometimes Mrs. S asked why I looked so happy.

How was I to tell her that my imaginary friend was a man who existed over 2,600 years ago, the man responsible for founding a religion? How was I to tell my second grade teacher the silly things Buddha was whispering in my ears about the other boys?

☙

Before Buddha became Buddha, he was a boy. He was Prince Siddhartha, heir to his father's throne, groomed to be the greatest king to ever live. And this was the pressure he lived with day in, day out. I imagine this to be stifling, every limb weighed down with lead. I imagine even Siddhartha, a boy destined for greatness, might crumble under that pressure.

The King sensed it too. He feared his son would leave the palace, so he built other palaces within the palace; there would be no need for Siddhartha to leave. But what was a boy to do without others around him?

I wondered about this.

When I was able to read, my mother gave me a book entitled *The Story of Buddha*. It was published by a press in India in 1978 and had pictures on every other page. What I remember most about the book were the times Siddhartha spent alone, something that displeased his father. The King bemoaned his son's disinterest in his education as king. He complained how Siddhartha would rather be alone in the garden than with his teachers.

But was he alone? Did he speak to the butterflies, the birds, the critters that scampered around in the green? Siddhartha, who possessed an extraordinary mind— could he have imagined someone in that garden with him, someone to talk to, to assuage his loneliness?

Possibly.

Later, when Siddhartha became Buddha, he would teach us that nothing is ever truly alone; everything is in relation to everything else.

☙

God is in everything. He is everywhere. He is always with you. Sitting with my wife's family at their Presbyterian church, I often hear these words, which are not dissimilar to the ones

I've heard when I was a boy sitting in temple listening to a monk's sermon. *Buddha is with you. Keep him in your mind and heart.* We look to these spiritual guides for ways to calm our tumultuous lives. There is comfort in the notion that we are never alone, that we are connected by an invisible thread to everything else in the world, the seen and the unseen.

જ

Buddha remained unseen when I travelled down the stairs in a laundry basket, one of my favorite games. But he was there, sitting with me. He remained unseen when we wrestled with body pillows. But he was there, with a pulverizing elbow. He remained unseen when I played with my action figures. But he was there, making my GI Joes move in combative maneuvers. He remained unseen when I played football outside. But he was there, my wide receiver, catching passes for touchdowns.

The real Buddha would not do such things. The real Buddha would have preached peace. The real Buddha would emphasize the life of the mind. But my Buddha was a mix of wisdom and mischief. He was a friend after all, and as a friend we were on equal ground, an amalgam of my thoughts and desires, and I desired a friend.

Still, this friendship, this very idea of him made me change, if only a little. Made me yearn for real companionship. And perhaps that was the reason I fought against my shyness, my anxiousness with others. If I could speak to Buddha, why couldn't I speak to the weird boy with the spiked hair, who looked just as lonely as I was. Or the other boy with the golden hair and thick glasses. Or the other boy who was gangly as a bean. And perhaps they had imaginary friends, too, and in this we shared something. And perhaps, our imaginary friends would not be needed anymore, had served their purpose, and now could simply disappear.

જ

At what moment he disappeared I do not remember. But he did, and so did the Buddha on the shelf one evening when

I was a teenager, and there was a new Buddha, a green Buddha, made of jade and covered in sparkling gold robes. This new Buddha was beautiful the way something new is beautiful, but I found myself looking for the familiar tarnish, the layer of dust that blanketed the old Buddha like new snow. The Buddha went when my father went; it was his after all, and was one of the only things he took with him after the divorce. I missed that old Buddha, my friend, missed his presence, his watchful gaze on that shelf. There were questions I still wanted to ask, guidance I still sought. I wonder what the view is like where he is now, and does he remember the boy who used to talk to him about his daily life? He sat there for fifteen years, and though Buddha had become Buddha again and not my play pal, he was never far from my mind. All I had to do was close my eyes and see him: his straight-back posture, his wide shoulders and narrowed waist, his elegant hands resting humbly on his lap.

The Cruelty We Delivered: An Apology

I

We didn't know what to do—your rocket energy sending Thai monks into fits, as they chased you through the Chicago temple, hands hiking robes like dresses, flip flops slapping callused heels. Your trouble made us roll our eyes and turn our back when you wanted nothing more than to pal around with us. You were a boy after all. So were we. But boys are cruel with neglect, crueler than the violence our hands are capable of.

II

We said cruel things, too. In our secret circle. In the temple library, where dust coated books about suffering, where furniture went to rot in the damp back room. Someone said, *He smells like barf.* Someone said, *Thai white trash.* I said, *No wonder his parents dumped him.* How could we know you hid behind a shelf of Buddhist books, patting a stray cat that made a nest in the hollow of a cabinet? How could we know what was to follow? If we did, would we have stopped our tongues?

III

He's lonely, your grandmother told us. She sold curry-grilled chicken and sticky rice on Sundays, like food carts in Thailand. After Buddhism class, we handed her crisp bills for sustenance. *Play with him*, she said, flipping drumsticks over on the grill, her hair kept under a shower cap. *Free food*, she said.

We were working class boys. Free was free.

IV

But your play was different. *Watch,* you said and launched a rock through a temple window. *Watch,* you said and trampled through the monks' vegetable garden, tomatoes staining your Converse. The monks would come then, your name a battle cry from exasperated mouths. What vows might they have broken if they caught you? You were, I'm sure, the thought that stirred them out of meditative moments.

We won't lie. It was funny: robed men in a mad dash after a sliver of a boy bounding bushes and Benzes. But your laughter—how can we forget that cackle that scattered crows?

V

Once, you showed us a kitten, a ball of grey in your dark hands. We circled you. We cooed. We tried to touch it, but you yanked it away, held it to your chest. *It misses its mother*, you said and delivered it back to its litter.

VI

Our parents said you hung yourself. This was years later when we got married and we had children and we lived in other parts of the world. We weren't surprised. We nodded. But I bet we thought about our cruelty and shrunk into ourselves.

I can't shake this image though: the time you stole holy water and dumped it over your head, the dripping glee on your face, your grin a half moon, your teeth blinding white. I remember that, my head hanging low, wishing forgiveness in the form of rain.

The In-Between Time

How I Tell the Story

So I woke up to the sound of a cat. We didn't have a cat. My mother and I were allergic to everything, especially a cat. But I heard one. Over my shoulder. It was the in-between time. My mother left for the hospital at 9:00, the night shift. My father came home from the tile factory at 11:30. I was alone till then. Behind me was the rest of my room: the squeaky computer chair; photos of my family, our lives preserved in frozen happiness. Above me was a portrait of Buddha, holy protector.

But the cat. I heard it.

So I opened my eyes and there was no cat. The chair, however, was squeaking. It always squeaked. It was the squeakiest chair in the neighborhood, the reason my mother didn't want to buy it at a garage sale, that and the duct tape over the tears in the brown leather. My father said this would be perfect for me. Said I could sit long hours and type my sixth grade papers. Said for $5 this was a steal. My mother said nothing but occupied herself at a table of used kitchen utensils.

But the chair. I heard it.

So I blinked. Blinked again. There was something or someone in the chair. A shadow. And it was rocking and squeaking. I want to say there was a shape to the shadow. I want to say there was a hat. I want to say that the shadow pointed its finger at me. I want to say all of this, but the truth was I ran out my bedroom door, hurried down the stairs and picked up the phone to call my best friend Kevin. I told him someone or something was in my room. I think I might have been crying. He told me his father was picking me up and to wait outside.

I waited and it was cold because it was winter in Chicago and my breath made white specters. When headlights drove up the driveway I waved and maneuvered myself into the back seat of Kevin's father's sports car—the Nissan 300Z—the first time I had been in a sports car. His father asked if I was all right. He said to wait here while he checked the house. Kevin turned from the front seat. He said, Dude. He said, Ghost? I nodded. He said, Cool. When his father came out minutes later, he shrugged but didn't say anything. Instead he backed the Nissan up and asked if I've ever gone fast before. When I shook my head, he gunned it, and I remember the force, an invisible shove and the deafening engine and the trembling under my feet.

What I Leave Out

That I woke up from a bad dream. I don't remember it. But it must have been loud because my ears were ringing from its aftermath.

That I had been reading Stephen King's *Salem's Lot*, a novel about vampires, and the book made me constantly look over my shoulder. When I closed my eyes, I felt fangs pierce my neck.

That I was a storyteller and prone to melodramatic moments. That I lied to get my way. That I lied to fit in. That I saw ghosts wherever I went because Thai people believed.

That every night I spoke to Buddha and God. I wanted to have them both. I had enough fears in the dark that two deities would have their hands full. I said, Buddha, protect me tonight. I said, God, watch over me. There was no need to tell my Buddhist parents about God. They had their own troubles.

That I woke up on Sunday, two days earlier, in the middle of the night to harsh whispers. I peeked outside my bedroom door towards the bathroom. My father was hunched over the sink, his arms supporting his weight, his head shaking—no— convulsing. My mother sat on the edge of the bathtub and pointed a sharp finger at him. She said he was crazy. *I ba!* His arms started to tremble. He raised his right hand in the air, and in it was a toothbrush. He raised his hand, as if he was about to strike my mother, who did not flinch, who remained vigilantly still. I must have made a sound because the two of them turned and smiled and pretended nothing was wrong. Did you have a nightmare? my mother said. I told her I did. I told her ghosts were chasing me and I couldn't get away.

What I Tell Myself

The fight was about toothpaste. For years, I thought this. Nothing ever angered my father to the point of rage. He spanked me only once and it was half-heartedly. He was known for his high-pitched hyena laugh, his charming smile. He was not like Kevin's father, who could bench-press my father with one arm. On his toes, my father stood five feet, six inches. His feet splayed in different directions. He drove a clunky Oldsmobile station wagon and listened to FM 100, soft elevator music.

But that night, he grew. He transformed. And the only reason I could think of for his anger was the lack of toothpaste. I had used the last of it. For days and weeks and years afterwards, I only squeezed a smidgen for myself, leaving enough for everybody else.

I told myself, It was the toothpaste. It must be the toothpaste. Always the toothpaste.

What I Imagined Happened

I have wondered for years what my father did when he arrived home from work and did not see me in bed, only my tousled blanket and my body pillow. Usually, he checked on me first thing, before sitting down to a late meal of ramen noodles or leftovers, before losing himself to an hour of late night TV. I would hear the back door open, and then his tired steps upstairs, and then the soft click of my door. Sometimes, he only peeked in. Sometimes, he hovered his hard hand over my head. I wondered about the panic that might have set in, how he went from room to room, closet to closet, attic to basement, calling my name with desperate urgency. I wondered at what time he called my mother at the hospital and what he might have said to her: *Our son is gone. I don't know where he is. Is he with you?* I could imagine her sudden breathlessness, her wide-eyed *huh?*, her mind playing the movie of herself backwards to the moment she left the house. *Did I lock the door? Did I check all the locks? Did I forget this one night?*

And here all their immigrant fears would become an actuality. They lost their son. In a foreign land. A land that did not make sense. The weather cold when it should be hot. People with rapid tongues. People with the capability of taking their only son. And here they would come together. Act together. Share each other's sorrow and shame and anger. Grieve together.

Or this:

Perhaps he heard the cat. The chair. Perhaps he saw the shadow. The hat on the shadow. Perhaps he turned on the light and chased the darknesses away.

Or, simply this:

How long did it take my father to find Kevin's father's note on the kitchen table?

The Next Day

At 6:30 in the morning, both my mother and father picked me up at Kevin's. My mother was in her nursing uniform and my father hadn't shaved. It was a school day and I still needed to get home, wash up, and get ready. The station wagon was warm. My mother squeezed my knee, but said nothing. My father looked at me through the rearview mirror. He asked if I slept well. I nodded. They didn't ask me about the night, and I was relieved. I wouldn't know what to say anyway because the truth had already begun turning in my brain.

Q: Did I hear a cat?

A: I think so.

Q: Did the chair squeak?

A: I'm not sure.
Q: Was I scared?
A: Yes.
Q: Did I want to flee the house?
A: Absolutely.

That Night

Kevin slept on a waterbed, and the two of us lay on it till past midnight. He asked for the story again and again, and each time the story grew and grew. Kevin came up with other theories. The house was haunted. The cat was also a ghost. The shadow was the former owner of the house—"Or! Holy Cow, it could've came with the chair!" I nodded at his enthusiasm, smiled at his excitement. "Only a ghost could give us a sleepover on a weekday," he said. But soon his father came down and told us to go to bed.

Kevin went to sleep quickly. His breaths came in gusty bursts. I stared at the ceiling. The undulations of the waterbed rocked me, made me feel adrift, floating through strange air.

Chop Suey

My mother was a champion bowler in Thailand. This was not what I knew of her. I knew only of her expectations of me to be the perfect Thai boy. I knew her distaste for blonde American women she feared would seduce her son. I knew her distrust of the world she found herself in, a world of white faces and mackerel in a can. There were many things I didn't know about my mother when I was ten. She was what she was supposed to be. My mother.

At El-Mar Bowling Alley, I wanted to show her what I could do with the pins. I had bowled once before, at Dan Braun's birthday party. There, I had rolled the ball off the bumpers, knocking the pins over in a thunderous crash. I liked the sound of a bowling alley. I felt in control of the weather, the rumble of the ball on the wood floor like the coming of a storm, and the hollow explosion of the pins, the distant crack of lightning. At the bowling alley, men swore and smoked and drank.

My mother wore a light pink polo, jeans, and a golf visor. She put on a lot of powder to cover up the acne she got at fifty. She poured Vapex, a strong smelling vapor rub, into her handkerchief, and covered her nose, complaining of the haze of smoke that floated over the lanes. My mother was the only woman in the place. We were the only non-white patrons.

I told her to watch me. I told her I was good. I set up, took sloppy and uneven steps, and lobbed my orange ball onto the lane with a loud thud. This time there were no bumpers. My ball veered straight for the gutter.

My mother said try again. I did, and for the next nine frames, not one ball hit one pin. Embarrassed, I sat next to her. I put my head on her shoulder. She patted it for a while and said bowling wasn't an easy game.

My mother rose out of her chair and said she wanted to try. She changed her shoes. She picked a ball from the rack, one splattered with colors. When she was ready, she lined herself up to the pins, the ball at eye level. In five concise steps, she brought the ball back, dipped her knees and released it smoothly from her hand, as if it was an extension of the floor. The ball started on the right side of the lane and curled into the center. Strike.

She bowled again and knocked down more pins. She told me about her nearly perfect game, how in Thailand she was unbeatable.

I listened, amazed that my mother could bowl a 200, that she was good at something beyond what mothers were supposed to be good at, like cooking and punishing and sewing. I clapped. I said she should stop being a mother and become a bowler.

As she changed her shoes, a man with dark hair and a mustache approached our lane. In one hand he had a cigarette and a beer. He kept looking back at his buddies a few lanes over, all huddling and whispering. I stood beside my mother, wary of any stranger. My mother's smile disappeared. She rose off the chair.

"Hi," said the man.

My mother nodded.

"My friends over there," he pointed behind him, "well, we would like to thank you." His mustache twitched.

My mother pulled me closer to her leg, hugging her purse to her chest.

He began to talk slower, over-enunciating his words, repeating again. "We … would … like … to … thank…"

I tugged on my mother's arm, but she stood frozen.

"… you … for … making … a… good … chop …suey. You people make good food."

The man looked back again, toasted his beer at his friends, laughing smoke from his lips.

My mother grabbed my hand and took one step toward the man. In that instant, I saw in her face the same resolve she had when she spanked, the same resolve when she scolded. In that instant, I thought my mother was going to hit the man. And for a moment, I thought the man saw the same thing in her eyes, and his smile disappeared from his face. Quickly, she smiled—too bright, too large—and said, "You're welcome."

The Wide-Open Mouth

I don't find photographing the situation nearly as interesting as photographing the edges.

~William Albert Allard, "The Photographic Essay"

O

The one piece of fame in my father's life: a picture of him, camera in hand, as the Queen of Thailand passes by. This moment happened in Chicago, at the Thai Buddhist temple, in the early eighties. Royalty did not visit our temple often, and it seemed like all Thai people in the Midwest congregated at this former Greek Orthodox Church, clogging up the residential streets off of North Hoyne Avenue.

My father was in a period in his life where he recorded everything, constantly carrying with him a Minolta X-700. On weekend excursions, he took that camera with him wherever we went and snapped pictures of my mother gathering golden delicious apples, or of me swinging a golf club, or of flowers. Lots and lots of flowers. My father was always looking for an opportunity to get rich quick. He bemoaned his time at the tile factory, and I believe he resented the fact that my mother was making more money as a nurse. He wanted something that would give him notoriety, something that he could brag about other than his golfing prodigy son. The temple photographer, a man whose name I do not remember, but whose face was skeletal with inflated eyes under thick glasses, had won top prize at a photography contest—fireworks over the Chicago skyline. He had won other prizes, too, a picture of monks meditating, a black and white photo of a little Thai girl trying to press the top button of a vending machine. This photographer was married to one of the most attractive women in temple, and my father, jealous of his success and popularity, thought that perhaps photography might bring him the same type of accolades.

It was not his photos, however, that he would be remembered for. It would be this picture, taken by the temple photographer on the day the Queen visited Illinois.

This photo hung in my parents' bedroom, above my father's aluminum desk. The Queen's right profile occupied the left side of the picture, blurry, as if she was part of a fading dream. But dead center was my father, in touching distance of Her Highness, clad in a blue gray suit, the same one he wore on his wedding in 1974, the only suit he owned, and large tinted glasses that made him look like a shifty poker player. And this we could not get over: his wide-open mouth.

O

The open mouth.

My mother, when she napped, would occasionally have her mouth wide open. I called it the fly catcher . . .

In a plane headed towards Thailand, my wife stares straight at me, mouth wide open. I wonder if she thinks *what a pitiful man I married*. When I ask her about the look, she says, "What look?" . . .

One time, I was playing tennis for my high school team, and it was an important doubles match against a rival school, when I saw the love of my life then—I don't recall her name, only her freckles—come to cheer me on after her choir practice. I stood wide-mouthed at the net, until the ball struck me in the armpit and stuck. Later, my doubles partner said, my mouth could've fit a planet.

O

The Minolta X-700 was one of the most popular cameras Minolta ever made. My father continuously bragged about its technology. He said it had a new flash metering device that automatically measured light. He spoke of exposure lock and focusing screens. He cradled the camera gently in his hands. I had never seen him hold anything so softly.

Usually, my mother would nod and listen; she was often patient with his excitement. This time his exuberance irritated her. "Perhaps," she said, "photography isn't the camera but the person holding the camera."

My father stood still for a moment, mouth tightly shut. Then he aimed the Minolta at her in the living room, the light coming softly through the sheer curtain, draping and darkening her face, her body silhouetted. He pressed the shutter.

O

It is an expression I have not seen from my father except for that picture. He is a man who possesses many faces, his cheeks and jowls elastic enough to display subtle degrees of emotions, including disappointment.

O

Eudora Welty: "A good snapshot stops a moment from running away." That was the problem with my father. He was famous for running away.

O

I was allowed to touch the camera once. My father was usually liberal with his possessions. I could hit rocks and apples with his golf clubs. I could take his leather briefcase and make it my own. I could wear his many Buddhas around my neck. The camera, however, was off limits because, once, when he first got the Minolta, I liked the sound the shutter made—a click with a CH—and the wind of the film advance lever. I repeatedly pressed the shutter and advanced the film, shooting nothing. When my father developed the film in the camera, most of the photos were blurred brown and green and one unfocused picture of a foot. From that day on, I was not to touch his camera.

Except one day at the zoo. My father had taken a picture of every animal. He was slow, waiting for the perfect still moment. But animals were animals and they operated by their own set of laws, not that of the artist. Nature photographer Frans Lanting says: "The perfection I seek in my photographic compositions is the means to show the strength and dignity of animals in nature." My father captured a monkey with a hard-on. My father captured a turtle hiding in its shell. My father captured a bird shielding itself with its wing. My father caught the back of a gorilla. Even when the subject remained static, like the python and boa constrictor in the reptile house, he could not figure out how to negate the glare from the glass.

At the end of the day, my mother suggested he take a picture of people. "Like, maybe, your son." He complied and took a picture of me pointing at the lion. He took a picture of me messing up my mouth with a good humor bar. He took a picture of me crying because I fell. Finally, I asked my father if I could take a picture of my mother and him. Reluctantly, he agreed, putting the camera strap around my neck and instructing me to hold the camera firmly in my hands.

"Just push the button," he said.

I pushed the button.

It was the last picture on the roll.

A couple days later, when my father picked up the film, the picture I had taken showed only my mother. The other half of the picture was black. A yellow streak like lightning split the center. The film hadn't advanced all the way, stuck at half of the frame. My mother smiled from under her great brimmed hat. Behind her was a pond that shot high into the air. Mallards and half of a swan swam back and forth. Kids with balloons and half of a balloon were in the distance. Some of my mother's shoulder was cut off. I could see part of my father's right hand.

O

We were on a golf course—we often were then—waiting for the group ahead us to finish the hole. It was a rare occasion of quiet. My father polished the lens of the camera. I sat beside him in the golf cart. He said I shouldn't wait for something to happen; I should make my mind up and just do it. I'm sure he meant to give me kind golfing advice, something on par with "Trust your instincts." He might have said "I love you" afterwards; maybe I'm wrong about that. But then he set the camera down and he squeezed my neck. I could feel the roughness of his skin, the hardened calluses under his middle finger and thumb, the easy pressure of his hand.

O

He told me other things, too. I have forgotten them though. I feel like a wide-open mouth.

O

I have been staring at the photo with the Queen for a while now—the actual photo and the one my mind has constructed. I am looking beyond it, looking into my father's wide-open mouth.

The photographer sees something—in this moment, in these few seconds—I have spent a lifetime trying to figure out.

This is not about the picture anymore.

Not about my father's mouth.

It never has been.

Look carefully, the photographer is saying. *Lean in close. It is there.*

O

At temple, after Sunday school, my father enrolled me in a photography class run by the temple photographer. I didn't want to do it. I would rather have played football with the other Thai boys. I would rather have been enrolled in kick boxing down the hall. I was one of two in the class. My father sat with me, the other student.

The temple photographer spoke of stillness. He spoke about photography like a monk talks about meditation. He said your hands can never shake. He said your eyes can never leave the viewfinder. He said a photographer, a real photographer, spends most of his time in the frame of a camera with one eye open. There was sadness in his voice when he said this.

He handed me his camera, heavy and bulky, a brand I don't recall, but something German.

My father spoke up. "Minolta is the best," he said.

The temple photographer nodded and smiled. He told me to aim the camera at my father and focus in on his face.

"Light touches," the photographer said. "Take your time."

I tried and tried.

"Tell me when your father becomes clear," he said.

My father remained fuzzy around the edges, his features blurry. I turned the lens back and forth. A bit here. A twist there. I did the best I could.

When I handed the photographer the camera, he looked through the viewfinder and shrugged. He said not to worry, but I should be a little softer next time.

My father patted me on the back. "It was the camera. Minolta is the best."

O

I worked at a camera store for a while that developed photos and sold equipment. The workers were divided into the photo developers and the sales people. I was a salesman because I looked good in a tie and had the gift of words. Like my father, I knew all the fancy technological terms so I could spout them at customers. It was all vocabulary though, because I didn't know how to take a good picture to save my life. My favorite cameras to sell were Minoltas. They gave wonderful sale incentives. Sell a Minolta advanced point-and-shoot and get $20-$50 on your check. No other company could match Minolta's incentive, especially Canon cameras, which gave you nothing.

A lot of the time, the photo developers would show us some of the wilder pictures—naked spring breakers, disgusting pranks, drunken costume parties. But my favorites were always the pictures of people caught unawares. Their mouths were always slightly parted.

O

In those seconds, what raced through my father's mind?
The Queen, the Queen!
What would it be like if I were king?
She's moving too fast, too fast, too fast . . .

O

Or perhaps, it was a lingering thought. Perhaps, at that moment, what weighed his hands down, what made him slow at the camera trigger, was the thought that I am here in the only suit I own, a tile chemist, not the rich entrepreneur I imagined I'd be, and my wife makes more money than me, and my son who loves me with his entirety thinks I am a legend, a superhero, and I'm afraid one day he will discover I am only a man with hard hands and wispy, impossible dreams.

O

My mother, too, has a picture with the queen. It's a black and white photo, and she is in front of Her Majesty, in her twenties, kneeling and receiving her degree from Siriraj Nursing School in Bangkok.

I found it in a box just yesterday.
It has never been hung up.

O

The Queen's picture is everywhere in Thailand. She is on billboards along roads. She hangs in every business establishment. She is in every house. Every Thai newspaper and magazine will publish at least five photos of her in each issue. She is often the focal point, the center of the frame. Her smile never tires. Her lips are always red. Her hair is immaculately in place.

One picture exists, however, where she is not the point of the picture, where she is just the foreground, and my father and his mouth have usurped her photographic power.

This picture the queen will never see because the temple photographer made only one copy and gave it to my family. He died shortly afterwards. Cancer. His beautiful wife took over his position, with her red nails and long hair and even longer legs. She wasn't as good. She spent too much time posing people and not enough time searching for moments.

O

My father laughed at the photo. He laughed and it echoed in our bi-level. He laughed and it rattled the pans in the kitchen. We laughed with him.

"Don't I look good?" he said.

"The best," we told him.

We laughed again.

"I look . . ."

" . . . like an orangutan," my mother said.

". . . like a golf hole," I said.

He shook his head.

"I look stupid." He laughed again, so hard he began to cry.

"Why didn't you take a picture?" my mother said.

He shrugged. "She came and went."

He went on to say he could feel the wind from her walk, and it felt like a blessing.

O

No, I am wrong. I have seen that look on my father's face one other time. When he left us. The snow covered the driveway. The brake lights lit the snow. The exhaust of his car billowed into the night sky. He had packed his car, and the two of us stood in the front hall, facing each other like cowboys before a draw. Only he couldn't meet my eyes.

"Where are you going?" I asked.

"Can't tell you."

"What's your phone number?"

"Can't tell you."

"When will I see you again?"

Then that look. Mouth like an egg.

For the Novice Bird-Watcher

I

When I was younger, if you had asked me to name three birds, I would have been hard-pressed to name one. Birds were categorized in an all-encompassing group: "Things that have wings and poop on my father's station wagon." Because I was born in the urban sprawl of Chicago, the only birds that mattered to me were the chicken and duck—I ate them with gusto—and the pigeons that pecked and waddled along busy city streets.

Once, while walking to Simmons Middle School, Tommy W kicked a pigeon into morning traffic where a bus nearly hit it. All I remember is the high-pitched squawk and the rapid blur of wings that carried the pigeon to the other side of 95th. Tommy and the rest of the boys laughed; I, too, was laughing, because Tommy scared me.

"Why did the pigeon cross the road?" Tommy said.

"Because you kicked the shit out of it," someone said.

More laughter.

Birds found a more significant place in my life that day, years before I married a bird lover, wore hi-tech binoculars around my neck, weighed my pocket down with a seven-hundred-page bird book, and took off into the woods, leaning my ears towards every chirp or rustle in the trees, because after school that day, I told my friends I had detention and they could walk home without me. But what I really did was scour the streets for that pigeon, to see if it was OK, to apologize. I didn't find it. Pigeons could look different and the same; they were part of the *Columbidae* family with three hundred different species around the world. I didn't know any of this, nor did I want to. My biggest concern was for the bird itself, for me too, who had spent the day grief stricken and fretting about its well-being. A sky rat, for god sake!

The best and probably most obvious lesson for any new birdwatcher is this: you have to love what you watch.

II

I was sitting on a park bench at one of the many Forest Preserves in Cook County. It was Sunday, and my family decided to come out for a picnic. Trips into the preserves were my favorite; being among so much green was such a dramatic change from the concrete and bricks of the neighborhood. Often, I hunted for frogs by the pond or counted the dragonflies that buzzed from one cattail to the next. This particular day, however, a small bird darted in and out of a nest in the dark cavity of some bushes, and I was transfixed. I don't remember the look of the bird, don't remember its color or its song, but I remember how it flew. Its small frame flapped its wings a few times and glided swiftly—dipping and darting, dipping and darting—until it came to a sudden rest on the ground or a branch or the antenna of a car.

This was its main purpose in life, flying, and the bird did it effortlessly, always returning back to the nest. I was five or six, and such things still captivated me. In a few years it would be remote control cars, and more years after that, the girl down the block who had a pretty nose, and it would be more years—after college, after being diagnosed with diabetes—that a bird in flight would seem fantastical again.

That day, however, flying was elementary.

Abandon all logic. Leap into the air. Soar.

Forget that you don't have feathers.

Forget Newton's Third Law and words like thrust and drag and kinetic energy.

When this bird flew, it just did it.

For an hour I sat there until my mother said lunch was ready and it was time to eat. I chewed absently, the bird still occupying my mind; it flew from one synapse of my brain to the next. It made me think that I could do it too, if only I believed hard enough.

I began flapping my arms. I cut through the air with ease. My T-shirt sounded, I imagined, like wings, like the snap of drying sheets on the line. I thrust my head upwards, hoping that simple movement would send me soaring above the trees. My mother and father watched me flap and thrust. Flap and thrust.

"Why do you look like an ostrich?" my father said in Thai.

"I think your son has gone crazy," said my mother.

"Blame it on America," my father said.

They laughed, but I didn't care.

Still flapping, I wondered what an ostrich was. I hadn't realized there were birds like penguins and emus and cassowaries and kiwis, birds that could not lift off the ground. Such information would have saddened me. A bird that could not fly? What was the point?

Furthermore, I had yet to realize that birds flew differently. Turkey vultures glided on air currents, circling and circling, wings outstretched like elongated fingers. And then there was the northern harrier I once observed while quietly sitting on a dock in upstate New York. This bird was a bad flyer. Sloppy in its execution. It looked as if it was out of control, at the mercy of the wind; its eyes were always aimed at the marsh, never at what was ahead, like me. And then there were the Canada Geese, whose flight is loud and systematic, the sky covered in Vs in the late fall. And what about the swallows whose swoops reminded me of acrobats?

To fly was as unique as an individual's walk, a pattern we fall into, a way of spotting one another. I can tell from a great distance that the person heading towards me is my wife with her steady stride, the strength in her lower half propelling her forward with unabashed confidence. Or my father, who has acquired the hunch and sadness of an old man, who walks like Death is waiting at the next bend.

That afternoon, I was trying to become an Ira Bird, the rare Thai-American variety that an avid watcher could spot during the summer months of 1981. This bird is now extinct, its life-span a few years long. One day, the Ira Bird was a bird, flapping his wings until he couldn't flap anymore, until he was breathless from the exertion. The next day, the Ira Bird matured and realized flight was impossible. But what he wouldn't give to be that bird again, to believe he might be able to fly! What he wouldn't give to possess the secret of flight.

III

Katie and I live tucked away in a small circular neighborhood. A three-acre forest of tall walnut trees shades our house, giving us the illusion that we have no neighbors, that we exist in the wild.

But we are far from being alone.

Around our cabin, we have created a metropolis. In the forest, woodpecker and chickadee houses are nailed to the thickest trees. On fence posts are rent-free apartments for swallows and bluebirds. Wrens live precariously in lofts hanging from the branches of our maple, and wild turkeys find shelter among the fallen trees in the forest, the slums.

Katie and I monitor the area like landlords. We watch for unwanted squatters—spiders, wasps, earwigs. When we find them, we are swift to evict.

In the front yard, under the river birch, we set up a cornucopia of restaurants: a log cabin replica holds sunflower seeds; a squirrel-proof feeder baffles and haunts our long-tailed critters; the woodpeckers cling to two green-wire suet feeders; the finches feast on a cylinder full of thistle seed; a glass hummingbird feeder brims with sugar water; and everyone drinks from the heated bird bath. These restaurants are sun-up, sun-down operations. The doves are the first to wake. They prefer fallen seeds. The Hairy and Downy woodpeckers find the suet and take turns pecking and eating. Then come the chickadees, who take one seed at a time and fly to a branch to eat it, and the gold and house finches that munch non-stop. The big guys arrive later. Cardinals and blue jays. Their presence chases the little ones away, but only for a bit. Eventually, they all come back and coexist.

There is not an exact count of how many birds there are on the planet, but most scientists believe the population exceeds 200 billion. In comparison, there are 6.7 billion people on earth. Simply: birds are everywhere. Every time I look into a tree or garden or university building or electric line, I am bound to see one. Yet, sometimes and somehow, they manage to escape my vision, even when we do look for them. Once in the mountainous jungles of Northern Thailand, Katie and I spent three hours on a trail bird watching. Out of those three hours, among the dense mossy trees and jungle vines, we saw no birds. We heard them—what sounded like hundreds of them—but despite our patience, they never showed themselves to us. How they remained invisible astounded me. I've begun to wonder whether this planet belongs to them, whether our log cabin is in *their* neighborhood, whether we are *their* tenants.

The birds that reside outside our cabin have become accustomed to our presence. In fact, they wait for either my wife or me to keep the feeders full and clean the bath every two or three days. They've become dependent on us, as we are on them. The chickadees fly at the window screen over and over to tell us there are no more seeds. The gold finches perch and wait. The doves coo. The woodpeckers peck at the cabin. And when we go out to replenish the food, they hide silently in the trees, watching us.

IV

When I was three, a baby cardinal fell from the nest after a strong Chicago gust, its wings starting to get brushes of red. It lay there on the stone path beside the garage, and my mother told me these things happened in life, and that we, too, would have to die. She held me to her leg, as I pressed the side of my face in the ruffles of her red dress. The image of the small bird, barely a bird, branded itself into my brain, and I couldn't stop staring, couldn't look away until my mother bent down and tossed the cardinal into our neighbor's wild rose bush, hundreds of pink petals and a tangle of thorns swallowing it up. Later that day, my mother told me that baby bird would live again. The bird-god Garuda would see that this cardinal found a better life, reborn in healthier circumstances. "It will learn to fly," she said. "So high and far, no one will touch it."

This gave me hope, and that hope became metaphor. When the next summer came, I pointed at the first cardinal I saw and asked whether that was the one that had fallen from the nest last year. The cardinal was a blurring streak of red, swooping in and out of my neighbor's apple tree, until it launched itself across the street, toward a sun that was setting like a half-eaten orange, and disappeared.

There were others that followed: the Downy woodpecker Katie found in the backyard of our old rented farmhouse in Carbondale, Illinois, after a vicious freeze, its color preserved like a painting; the unknown bird that collided into my windshield; the mallard that tried to cross the Interstate; the sparrow that could not escape the orange cat's grasp.

I hold onto the image of birds—in death or in flight.

"She soared through the sky like a bird," my students often write, and though I have seen the line hundreds of times, have spoken often about clichés, this one I let slide. The image remains fresh, and in that simple simile, they are describing more than the physical sensation of weightlessness; they are transcending the boundaries of human law and physics, bounding into a lyrical and surreal world that expresses their deepest desires, carried on the wings of an immortal bird.

V

When we have killed all that is alive on our planet, when debris erodes away, and what is uncovered is a new green, the birds will come back. They will fly from distant planets or emerge from the deepest, clearest ponds this world has ever known. There will be billions of them, each a different color and size, birds that exist only in our imaginations. Fire crowns, sleek silver bodies, beaks pointed like a needle. In this new world, no one will name them; no one will keep them in cages. They will start anew. They will sing so loud the planet will rumble along in melodic pleasure.

Wild Boys. Chicago Boys. Dumb Boys.

We strode off into the city, as if we owned it. This part of it, at least—the southside—with factories spouting off plumes of smoke, old brick houses weathering Chicago winds, endless strip malls where historical churches used to be, and an airport so close we thought we could touch the underside of planes. We said things like: "Wild, man," or "Dude, let's get wild," or "It's a jungle out there." We sported the southside uniform, an homage to late '80s long-haired bands like Mötley Crüe, and Skid Row, and Guns N' Roses: our holey jeans, our badass bandanas hanging out of our back pockets, our white T-shirts with crass, clever sayings like "Just Do Me," our heavy as hell Doc Marten boots, unlaced and scuffed, scraping the concrete when we walked—no—swaggered, like limp noodles.

And there was concrete. Everywhere. Chicago is king of it. Concrete was the foundations of homes and skyscrapers. Concrete walls kept interstate noise away from neighborhoods. Capone buried people in concrete. Concrete blocks were tied to bodies and tossed in the Chicago River. Concrete driveways, concrete sidewalks, concrete business offices, concrete poles and pillars and school steps. Concrete crumbled into dust in our hands and made us feel like we possessed superhuman powers.

Here, in this urban landscape, everything was concrete . . . *and* tar and metal and sound: car horns, squealing busses, construction workers, construction, the buzz of electricity like a hummingbird in flight. Sound, there was no absence of it; not even during the night because the city can't stand silence, the city is afraid of it—a quiet moment. Because if the city is quiet, something is deathly wrong.

Our wildness, our wilderness, was the long city blocks with streets named after a Polish war hero, a Roman philosopher, a politician: Pulaski, Cicero, Kedzie. Forest of fast food joints, all-night Greek diners lit up in neon. And the prairie of car dealerships: Ford, Oldsmobile, Chevrolet; red hot balloons tied on the antennas of used cars or an inflatable, gigantic King Kong on top of the dealership building, the one that we popped with a bb gun so it looked like a black melted mess.

We owned the malls—Chicago Ridge, Ford City, Evergreen—rode the escalators at Sears and JCPenny's, put mannequins in compromising positions. We ate at the places our friends worked at and macked on hotties every chance we had. We said things like "macked" and "hotties" because our language was wild, born from working class roots, shaped by rough and tumble tongues. We clipped the end of words, which formed deep in the back of the throat, deeper still, in the gut. Sometimes what came up was not so much a word but a grunt, a growl.

We were Chicago boys. Wild Chicago boys, but we never said boys. We said men, because men had power, and power was what we wanted. Boys played in the city playgrounds. Men smoked in the city playgrounds. Boys slid on the slides. Men peed on the slides. And we were men, no older than fifteen or sixteen. Power made us travel in packs like hyenas. People said when we passed, "There goes a wild bunch," or "Those boys are wild," or "They get wilder each year."

But there were the hiding spots too, in this urban jungle. The graveled back allies. The foot-wide spaces between garages where we stashed our father's whiskey, cigarettes, and porn.

Our wilderness was not static like the Illinois fields hours south of us. "That shit's boring," we'd say, and spit like we knew any better. Our landscape moved and changed and was dictated by commerce and capitalism. One day there would be a hot dog shop and the next it would become vitamin store. One day the building on 95th, the gray one with the clock tower, stood tall and imposing, the next day it was leveled and the day after that it was a concrete parking lot. Shocker.

To exist here was to live with the knowledge of an ev-er-evolving urban landscape. Attachment was detriment. Heartbreak was inevitable. And some of us knew it too well already. Some of us were raised by single mothers. Some of us were beaten down by our daddies. Some of us were simply lost. Our landscape changed like the streetlights. Our land-scape was the streetlights. But it was always green, and we were always speeding.

We understood there was a hierarchy to things. We under-stood our parents came first. Then our teachers. Then men in uniforms. But we wanted to usurp the police, who were not the police to us. They were *bacon, pig, copper, five-oh, po-po, swine,* and *whitey.*

Most of us were white—Polish or Irish—except for me. But I was called the other white meat.

One day, we stood on the overpass on Southwest High-way, a hiding spot, an urban treehouse, in front of Oak Lawn Community High School, dropping apples on cars below. We didn't care about accidents; we didn't care about injuries or car damage; we didn't care about anything but the supposed power we wielded. Our thoughts never went beyond action. Stupidity made us forget consequence.

An apple thudded on a trunk, a windshield, a hood, and we hid as cars honked and swore or just drove off as if nothing happened.

"Wild," we said.

We said other things too, like, "Wicked." Or "Gnarly." Or "Wicked gnarly."

When a pig in a pig mobile was about to drive under our overpass, one of us said, "I dare you."

Another said: "Piggy wiggy."

Another said: "Bacon, bacon, bacon," like that dog treat commercial.

I grunted, which meant, I'd do it. I dropped the apple, watched it fall and splatter on top of the squad car.

This was our shared moment. Our way of owning this land, this territory. Our way of marking. Because we believed we owned people, too, like that stupid pig in his stupid pig car. "What a Sally," we said. And we wanted to say other things, and we wanted to high five each other.

The car stopped. The lights came on.

We were off. Our legs carried us down the overpass stairs, skipping three or four steps at a time, past the gas station and minimart, past the car dealerships and the deflated King Kong, past the 24-hour Greek diner, and past the McDonald's, past concrete and concrete and concrete. Our Doc Martens were slamming on it. The squad car closed in. I turned to look at my friends, and we weren't "we" anymore. Mike said, "Oh shit, oh shit, oh shit." Matt said, "My mom's going to kill me." Danny Boy didn't say anything and was crying.

On 93rd, each one of us scattered in different directions, blackbirds in frightened flight.

I knew the neighborhood. Because I studied it. Because when you're fifteen or sixteen, all you do is cruise, even if you don't have a car. You cruise the avenues, the alleys. You cruise yards and cracked sidewalks. You cruise on top of rooftops. Cruising is what boys did. Because you never know when you would need to utilize those secret spots, like that afternoon.

I turned into someone's yard.

Jumped someone's fence.

Breezed past someone's child hopscotching in her driveway.

Bounded over someone's hedges.

Trampled through someone's garden.

Hurdled someone's Jesus statue.

Until I was home.

I watched out the front window the rest of the day, expecting a squad car to swing up my driveway, its lights flashing red and blue on the white siding of my house. I waited for the doorbell to ring, for a man with a gun at his side and a gold badge on his chest to cuff me and take me away, and I wondered what would happen to me then, what punishment would befall me, this Thai boy, this Chicago boy, this other white meat, who stupidly tested his powers and found out he had none.

Consequence

In my Cub Scout pack, I was the poison ivy alarm. Out of all the lessons at den meetings, this was the one I most remembered. Our Den Mother had pointed to pictures of three broad leaves and told us tales of people who came in contact with them. One time, she told us, a friend of hers went into the woods to do number two and accidentally brushed his bottom on poison ivy. Hours later, rashes and bumps broke out all over his skin and he couldn't stop scratching to the point she had to take him to the hospital.

Her story stuck with me. I was allergic to everything already, miserable during hay fever season, another thing I inherited from my father whose allergy sneezes shook the earth. There was nothing more uncomfortable than a constant itch, one that gnawed at you and didn't go away no matter how much you scratched.

When my father came to the Father & Son Cub Scout Halloween celebration at Maple Lake, a forest preserve in Cook County, Illinois, he wanted to know what poison ivy looked like. It was the first time he took part in one of my extra-curricular activities. Usually, he worked at the tile factory most of the afternoon, so I rarely saw him except for weekends. That day, my father was in navy blue slacks, white leather shoes, and a pink golfing polo. He did his best to converse with the men, who towered over him, but most conversations led to uncomfortable silences.

Apart from being a small Thai immigrant, my father was different from other fathers. Other fathers wore rugged jeans and work boots. Other fathers sported camouflage jackets and hats. Other fathers gripped cans of Budweiser and smoked unfiltered cigarettes. My father did not fit that mold, and because I was seven and a Cub Scout, an organization of boys training to be men, I wondered if my father was a man. I wondered if the other kids thought I was like him.

In one of the activities, my father and I entered the forest to forage for things to decorate our lopsided pumpkin: pretty stones, twigs, fallen leaves, acorn tops, strips of tree bark. So when he asked me what poison ivy was, I located some at the base of a maple.

My father pointed at it. "Are you sure?"

I understood his question. For a plant to be called poison ivy one expected it to *look* poisonous or alien, like the Venus Flytrap. But to the untrained eye, poison ivy looked no different from other bushes and shrubs and trees. It did not drip purple ooze or emit a foul odor. It was green and red and leafy like everything else around us.

My father knelt beside it and pointed at it again. "This poison ivy?"

"Yes," I said.

He moved to touch it, his finger hovering over the plant.

"What are you doing?" I said.

"Want to know what happen. Want to know if really poison."

"You're not going to like it." I couldn't stop him. He touched it. He pinched a leaf, tore a bit of it off, and brought it to his nose. He sniffed.

"I no feel anything." He wiped his hands on his slacks.

There was a chance that my father was among the twenty percent who were immune to poison ivy. But from what I remembered reading, it took some time before the skin got irritated by the oils of the plant. He shrugged and laughed, and I shrugged and stood a good distance away from him the rest of the time we collected our items, telling him to wash his hands in the creek bed so I wouldn't be infected too.

When we started decorating the pumpkin, I noticed a bump on my father's cheek. As I stuck thick branches into the top of the pumpkin—its antennae—I noticed another. As I pushed acorn tops around the stem of the pumpkin, my father began to scratch a collected series of bumps that started at the corner of his mouth and ended near the point of his chin. As I glued on leaves for the pumpkin's multicolored hair, he was scratching so hard, tiny bubbles of blood emerged from his skin.

"Dad," I said, pointing at his face, trying not to draw the attention of the other fathers and sons around us. His fingers scratched and scratched. Blood smeared his face. But he kept working, kept shoving acorn tops into our pumpkin. He carved wavy lines on the sides and inserted leaves into the space. He told me the pumpkin's eyes should be the weathered stones from the creek, the smooth brown ones that were thin and long. When we were done, our pumpkin looked like an Asian alien bellowing blessings from its large oval mouth.

We took first place for our pumpkin. We would take first a month later with the regatta boat we built together and first again for the best meal cooked by campfire during the winter campout. That day, with the blue ribbon in my hand, my father drove home, grinning like a jack-o-lantern, his rash already scabbing up. I wanted to tell him I told you so. But it seemed he knew what I was thinking and said that there were some things you must find out yourself, no matter the consequence. "Understand?"

I did.

I reached up and touched his skin.

Constellations

And—I'm just realizing this—memory is what peo-
ple are made out of. After skin and bone, I mean.
And if memory is what people are made out of, then
people are made out of loss.

–Bill Roorbach

I

I used to connect my mother's freckles with my fingers.
Sometimes, I traced stars. Sometimes, a smiley face. Despite
her reprimands—"It sin to touch mom head"—she did not
pull away, but allowed my finger to travel at will. I marveled at
the smoothness of her skin. For every dot, I expected my finger
to glide over a bump, an imperfection, like my father's large
mole that looked like a fattened tick on his chin. I often asked
why other Thai moms didn't have freckles. I asked her where
mine were. I don't recall what she said. What I do remember,
as my finger went from dot to dot, was her asking, "What you
draw today?"

II

It comes at peculiar times, the smell. During a stroll to the
mailbox or in the parking lot behind the Chinese buffet. But
when it comes, it lingers and spreads and awakes every sense.
It is not a pleasant smell, not like the ones my grade school
teachers put on my homework—their candy-scented markers,
their scratch-n-sniff stickers. It is the smell of artificiality, of
chemicals, of lost things.

III

These are the things that stick:

. . . chopsticks, black rubber hose, Aunty Sue's gun, Michael Jackson, boxing glove, dead mouse, Kangol caps, forged signatures, golf ball, upstairs Buddha, Hulk Hogan, Chinese stars, Michigan apples, envelope full of twenties, salt water, microwaved hot dogs, the arrow of light . . .

IV

"Ask Buddha for success. Ask Buddha for everything."

V

I can't help but feel I've forgotten something. It was important, too. It was something that would have made me smile. The more I think about it, the more I feel it slipping away—that picture, that moment. It might come back. Someday. Recalled through some image. The space between tree branches. The whistling of the teapot. The zig-zagging rabbit. The scent of mothballs. I hope it will make it back. I don't want to lose anymore.

VI

The morning I woke up and found she was gone I wandered all over the house and called out for her. My aunt said I sounded like a sheep. She said I repeated mother in Thai over and over.

"Mae," I said. "Mae."

I even gathered my courage and went into the crawl space, a room I never ventured into without her. We kept the things we no longer needed down there—garbage bags full of toys, toasters, clothes. It was a dark and cold place. Pipes ran above my head. The uneven pavement made my knees hurt. The shadows in the back moved.

"Mae," I said. "Mae."

The back of the crawl space frightened me. That was where my mother hung coats along a water pipe. They moved, those coats. They swayed in some draft. The plastic around them made noises.

"Mae," I said. "Mae."

But that day I did go back, despite my fear. I pushed on. I spoke louder, hoping my voice would quiet my fright, so loud I began screaming at nothing but coats from many winters ago. Suddenly, the smell of mothballs rose around me.

VII

But I like it, the smell. Like I enjoy salt water on canker sores or endlessly picking at scabs or plucking nose hairs. I enjoy it because at the exact moment I smell it, my imagination smells something else, something far away. And in that instant, the world and its infinite possibilities open up again.

VIII

There's more:

. . . holy incense, spring rolls, duck heads, boxed mashed potatoes, bitter melon, Kevin's divot chest, Nintendo, watermelon rind, Alyssa Milano, sex manual under parents' bed, maple leaf in book, family portrait taken at Sears, dildo . . .

IX

This was our game: *Hold your breath until we pass the cemetery, OK?* my mother said. *Do not wake the dead.* There was one traffic light along that stretch on Ridgeland Avenue and other variables that made the game difficult—rush hour, accidents, police waiting with the radar to catch speeders. Without any of these, the cemetery already stretched for thirty seconds. With any of these, it could go beyond a minute, sometimes two.

Once, we hit all the variables plus a red light. I held my breath. I held it until I turned red then blue then purple. I watched my face change color in the ghostly reflection of the car window. My mother held her breath, too, beside me in the back seat. Pain never entered her face. She did not change color. Her eyes were closed. Her chest was still. She looked peaceful, like a corpse. That was the reason I let my breath out. I thought she had actually died. I thought I had lost her. When I gasped for air, her eyes popped open and she smiled and said, *They will come for you.*

X

No matter what I've told you so far, every attempt to get back has failed.

XI

She came back, and for the next week, I did not stray far from her. Wherever she moved, I followed close behind. I feared losing her again, losing her forever. Something about her had changed. She moved gingerly, her hand always at her mid-section, her back slightly hunched over. She did not sleep in the bedroom upstairs, but on the pull-out bed on the first floor. When I tried to hug her, my aunt said to take it easy, to be gentle.

The first night she was back, I asked, "Where did you go?"

"Hospital."

"Are you dying?"

"No," she said

"Why did you go?"

She lifted her shirt to show me the bottom half of her belly. It was the largest scab I had ever seen, a narrow one that went from one end of her stomach to the other. There were uneven stitches in it. It looked like the sizzled millipede on the concrete in Bangkok. I wanted to run my finger along her stitches just so I'd know what it felt like.

She told me I couldn't. Infection.

"Does it hurt?"

She shook her head and lowered her shirt. During the rest of the month, whenever I asked, she always showed me.

XII

Buddha does not answer prayers. He offers suggestions. All of them will lead you far from here.

XIII

I drew a Beetle, with my finger, on her face. Not the insect but the car. We had a light blue one that we traded for a station wagon the color of dirt. I liked the new car because I could sit in the back and make faces at people in traffic, but I found I missed the Beetle and the puttering muffler. I missed it even though I fell out of it once, while my aunt pulled out of the Dunkin' Donuts parking lot—powder on my face, blood on my cheek. I missed the Beetle so much I traced it in her freckles.

When I was done, I made it move. The Beetle sped across the bridge of her nose, down the steep slope of her chin, and then wound back around to rest on her earlobe.

"Nowhere to go?" My mother, on the pull-out, kept her eyes on a Thai soap opera magazine. "Car stuck?"

"Just resting," I said.

XIV

There are wounds that heal slower than others, and sometimes not at all. Sometimes they leave marks. The black fly bites, the pencil-stab scar, the laceration on the big toe after the fall. Memories etched into the body. Marks that won't allow forgetting.

XV

And there was the time I was riding my bike, a junky speedster bought at the flea market. It was red, I think, a delicious red like the stripes on a candy cane. I pedaled hard toward home, my legs pumping faster and faster, and I thought this was what it felt like to fly. When I made the turn into my driveway, one of the cracks that had gotten larger and larger over the years, caught the front wheel of the tire. I was *truly* flying then. I put my arms out in front of me. I imagine I looked like Superman, my hero, but I didn't feel like him. I felt out of control. In the seconds to come, even then, I knew that when I hit the ground it would hurt. The strange thing, however, in my memory, I don't remember what happened after I landed. I don't remember the impact. I don't remember whether my mother came out of the front door. I don't remember what she said to soothe my crying. I don't remember how she tended to my wounds. The memory—the true memory—is of sudden flight.

XVI

There were boxes of them in every corner of the house, like little white edible marbles. They were placed in drawers, in closets, even in the fireplace. Everywhere you turned, if you looked carefully, you would be able to see them. I never thought this strange.

Once when a friend drove me home after a party, he said, "It is weird, Ira, not to see any moths around your house in the summer. Not even around the lights."

XVII

This is someone else's story.

Once he said there was a moth that was a foot wide, wings like a bat, and it flapped and hovered around the front porch light. The wings were transparent. When it flapped, it made wind. How the thought of burning it entered his head, I do not know. But that was what he did. He threw some lighter fluid on it. Watched it flap on the concrete and then lit it. He said it took off one more time before disappearing into smoke. There was nothing left of it, but the outline of its charred body on the concrete—its wings like the ears of Buddha.

XVIII

I wonder what has left already, disappearing in the folds and cracks of the brain.

XIX

. . . salted fish, plastic Xmas tree, Matchbox cars, sewing machine, whistling teapot, downstairs Buddha, ninja shoes, fish heads, family portrait taken in Thailand, blue Bic pen . . . .

XX

I wasn't a loud crier. I had long since learned that crying sometimes did more harm than good. But the fall hurt. The shock of hitting the ground stole my breath for a few seconds, and when I gasped for my first lungful of air, tears started spilling off the sides of my face. I didn't move. I kept silent. I stared through the branches of my neighbor's apple tree, at the patches of blue above me. In my hands, I still held the tree limb that used to hold my weight. It was thick like a fat water pipe. I used to pull myself up and into the tree by that limb, into the cradling trunk. A few apples dropped to the ground beside me, and maybe that alerted my mother—their solid *thunk*s on the grass.

When she came out, she was in her pajamas, a red gown that was cool to the touch and went to her ankles. She didn't see me at first. She said my name over and over. Another apple fell. On my forehead.

She was quick then to scoop me up. She touched every part of my body, asking me what hurt. I told her nothing hurt, but the place where the apple hit. She asked me to wiggle my fingers. Wiggle my toes. She asked me to walk.

Pleased that I was all right, she held me close and told me I was too big to climb trees. She told me, in time, I would forget all of this.

II

Back against the wind. Face to the land.

–Thai Proverb

Floating Family

We are on the Gunnison River in central Colorado, the sky darkening from the south, thunder clapping in the distance. A drizzle begins to fall. The wind picks up.

I have already gone in. Not a minute on the innertube, my 300-pound body flipped over a white boulder jutting out of the river like a shark fin. I banged my knee against the rock. The water shocked the breath out of me. I swiveled back on the tube, drenched and irritated, knee throbbing.

This was Katie's idea, a relaxing excursion on the river. This was my first vacation with her family. Katie and I had been fighting about the amount of time she didn't spend with me. I am an only child, the center of attention. I was trying to find my footing in a family who believed in God, a family who ate mashed potatoes instead of jasmine rice, a rural family, not used to a kid from the southside of Chi-town, who had never ridden a horse until a week ago. I'm still picking pine needles from my hair.

It's been raining the last few days and the water level is high and moving fast. Katie floats far ahead. She tilts her head back, her hair flowing over a yellow innertube, her body limp and relaxed. Her older brother, John, unsuccessfully maneuvers a cheap blowup raft bought on clearance at Walmart, spinning in circles. Dinny, Katie's mother, sixty-three with bad legs, steers a rickety canoe, trying to find a place to cast for trout.

But weather moves in. Heavy drops of rain pelt my glasses. A hard wind blows the canoe into low-lying trees, the tip of it stuck in roots and branches. Dinny sticks her oar into the river, steadying the boat. She tries to paddle out, but the swift current keeps her locked in.

Lightning jags across the sky.

Dinny waves her oar in the air. She's in trouble.

"Yo, John," I scream. John is spinning. "Your mom's stuck." I see his face and then his back. Face then back.

"OK," he says, and the fireman in him kicks in. He gains control of the boat, steers it to shore and leaps out, running upstream.

"Katie!" My voice doesn't reach her. I whistle and she raises her head. I give her a thumbs down, then wave my hand toward the shore. She understands.

A rocky inlet splits the river temporarily into two. I paddle my hands towards it. When I stand, my knee buckles; it has swelled to double its size. I balance on one leg.

John walks across the river. He takes one slow step at a time, the water above his knee. He is immovable like a rock. Dinny extends her oar and pulls him to the canoe. He dislodges the front from the trees and jumps in, taking command from behind. With three quick paddles he's at the inlet.

"My knee's pretty bad," I say.

"Get in," John says. Another streak of lightning. "We need to get off the river."

"It'll tip," I say, thinking of the three other times I've been in a canoe.

"This one's un-tippable," Dinny says.

I trust her. John ties the innertube to the canoe. It floats behind us.

The rain comes down so thick none of us see the rock until we hit it. The front of the canoe rises and tips over. Oars, fishing poles, tackle box, extra life jackets, a red T-shirt, a florescent green baseball cap, an umbrella drift past me.

Dinny begins to float away, her body submerged in the river, only her head breaking the surface.

I rise out of the water and dig my feet into the rocky riverbed. I grab Dinny's shirt collar and keep her from floating away.

"I got her," I say.

"He does," says Dinny.

"All right," says John, shouting over the sound of rain, over the moving waters. He rights the canoe. "Let's do this again."

"We lost a lot of stuff," I say.

"Just things," says Dinny.

This time John makes it to shore. Katie has corralled hippie boys who live in a cabin off the river to help us pull the water-logged canoe in. They place towels around our shoulders. The frigid water has numbed my knee.

"Balls out," says one of them with hair like hemp.

Wrapped in a towel, Dinny takes my hand and says thank you. "No problem," I tell her, looking down the river. I imagine the things we lost, the current carrying them away, bobbing up and down, riding the clear surface.

The Takeover: A Love Story

In memory of Normagene Warner

The Penultimate

We woke to the sound of them behind the walls, scratching frantically for an escape into the warmth of the house. Our two golden retrievers followed the sound and then began running back and forth from one end of the bedroom to the other, noses sniffing like a chugging train, rhythmic and relentless. Mick, the sportier of the two, bared his teeth once at the white wall and let out a warning bark at whatever was inside. He was doing what was in his instincts, protecting us, the two who rubbed his belly and gave him cheese whiz before bed.

The scratching came at the same time every day: 6 A.M. It was our alarm clock.

One summer morning, Katie rolled over and stared at the ceiling. She hated for her sleep to be disrupted, always proclaiming she needed at least eight hours to be useful to anyone.

"I think they want the house back," she said.

A Time Before

The farmhouse was white and rustic, dating back before 1918. It was located on the edge of Carbondale, a city near the southernmost tip of Illinois, where the landscape began to change from the flat farmland that pervaded the middle part of the state to undulating hills and thick forests. There were still places, however, where the land flattened out and the sky loomed large overhead.

Inside the house, the kitchen was redone—new cabinets put in, new linoleum on the floor. Floral print wallpaper wrapped around the room—not the kitschy country type—but one that immediately set you at ease. The upstairs was the oldest part of the house. There were holes in the wooden floor; some looked down into the dining room, and one focused on the entrance to the master bedroom. Despite its flaws, the upstairs came with a newly installed half bath and a reading nook that afforded the best views of the yard and the field beyond. It was easy to lose yourself up there, easy to imagine you were in another time.

"It's old," Katie told me in my one-bedroom apartment only an undergraduate could stand. This was a few years before we were married. We weren't anything but friends then, friends who had begun to obsessively hang out with each other.

She drove to the house at nine at night and said she could barely see it, only its ghostly outline. She didn't even know the color. What she was certain of, after weeks of fruitless searches, was that this house was the one. She knew even before the sunlight hit the white siding and stirred the birds awake under the umbrella branches of the spruce, that she had found where she—we—would spend the next four years of our lives.

It wasn't the house, however, that appealed to Katie. She pulled onto the gravel path of McDaniel Drive and wound her way towards the house, leaving a trail of white behind her. McDaniel dead-ended at the house. Before reaching it, two hickories on either side of the drive branched overhead.

This was the gateway. This separated us from the outside world.

Driving up, Katie noticed small and dilapidated buildings—old chicken houses, a two-car garage that had clearly once been a barn, a shed, an outhouse. A twisting magnolia stood in front of the house. It was early spring and the magnolia had begun to bud.

The fields called to Katie, the openness, the way the land dipped and stretched in the distance. Even at night, there was an endlessness about the land, and the eye could travel on forever without bumping into a tree, a house, a person; it could continue to stretch until the land looped back to where she was standing—at the edge of this infinite unused field, the crickets and spring peepers announcing the coming of a new season.

There, at the edge of that field, Katie was not Katie anymore. She was a farm wife. And it was not 1998, but 1918. And the chickens were stirring. And the clothes on the line swayed in the breeze. And the indigo bunting took flight from one tree to the next. And the view, from where she stood, was the same.

ↁ

Such openness scared me. I was a child born and raised by Thai immigrants in Chicago, and I reveled in finding hiding places. There were so many secret spots in the city. If you kept your back to the wall and your eyes wide you could see danger coming. *It* could come from anywhere. Be ready. But that was the problem. The danger was an elusive *It*, and *It* also knew how to hide. *It* was savvy and shapeless. *It* was nothing tangible, just a tangle of irrational worries. Because of this, I was on guard there most of my life.

When I first saw the farmhouse, a couple weeks before Katie was to move in, I told her she might tell her landlord to install new locks on the doors.

She gave me one of those looks I have grown accustomed to, one that intimated that what I had said bordered on the absurd. "Why?"

"Anybody could break in."

"No one will break in," she said.

"How can you be so sure?"

"Because."

"But there are bad people out there."

"There're bad people everywhere. I have dogs."

She did, but I could see Mick and Bonny licking an intruder to death before I could see them biting one.

"Trust me," Katie said. "Nothing will happen."

She, of course, was right.

The word "trust" stayed with me, though. This was the difference between Katie and me. She came from a world of trust, a childhood in central Illinois where the doors were always unlocked. I came from just the opposite, one where my mother and I did nightly checks of all the locks in our suburban bi-level. Over the weeks and months of our friendship, however, I had begun to trust Katie, more than I had ever trusted anybody, and she was slowly peeling away my distrust, showing me that trust can come from a number of things, even the land itself, even in this rented old farmhouse.

I could see the faith she had in this house and its surrounding property, the lightness in her step as she walked through the yard and marked off areas where she would plant bulbs and annuals and roses, or when she ventured into the fields with the dogs, the grass as high as her hips, and the goldens leaping and disappearing, leaping and disappearing. There was a bond she had with the land that I could not comprehend. She understood the nuances of the wind, the whisperings of the trees, the howls of the coyotes. At times, when Katie was far in the fields, she disappeared, as if the land had taken her in.

∽

One day, I found myself standing at the front door, looking and waiting for something or someone to approach. Squirrels scrambled across the yard. Deer stood in the field. Once a car drove up McDaniel and it must have realized it had come the wrong way, so it backed up before reaching the house. Other than that, no one came uninvited.

A few hours later, I abandoned my post.

∽

After work, I didn't go back to the apartment, but headed the ten minutes out of town to the farmhouse. In those ten minutes, I left behind the strip malls, the department stores, the fast-food chains, and soon, I was passing empty fields, grazing palominos, houses that were spread apart and had rows of rural mailboxes across the street. The drive to Katie's captivated me in a way I had never experienced before, or, at least, I never took notice. I assumed that if there were no buildings, no lights, no McDonald's, no incessant beeping of cars, no cars at all, then there was nothing of worth to look at, nothing to pay attention to. It was a city prejudice, I realized, one that often prompted Katie to call me, "City boy," but on those drives, I looked forward to that particular quiet and emptiness.

At the house, I helped Katie with whatever she needed help with. She asked my opinion about where to position her furniture, where to hang her photos and posters, and what part of the house received the most light so she could lay out her houseplants. I helped her dig the garden, the earth thick and layered and dense. I was so involved in putting her house together I had begun to feel like it was mine, also.

I wasn't the only one.

When Bill and Normagene Warner, the landlords, stopped by to see how Katie was settling in, they immediately assumed I was her boyfriend, which I didn't deny right away. I wondered what they would make of me, an Asian kid out in the middle of nowhere; you just didn't see us outside city limits. But Bill and Normagene, they were good people. Bill, a gentle giant and retired minister, shook my hand, his grip solid for a man in his seventies, and Normagene held onto Bill's arm, steadying herself on the uneven gravel driveway. This had been Normagene's childhood home, and she told Katie and me what she loved about it.

"The fireflies," she said. "They come in the summer and it's like a bunch of little lights rising from the ground. They are an absolute treat, I assure you."

"I bet," Katie said. "I love fireflies."

"And if you put feeders out, you'll get all kinds of birds. Do you have feeders?"

"A few," said Katie.

"Make sure you have hummingbird food, too."

"I've never seen a hummingbird," I said.

"Then that's another treat."

Katie and I smiled. Bill kept quiet and amiable.

"And I don't want to forget to tell you about the rhubarb behind the garage. I just love rhubarb. So did Mama. She made the best rhubarb pie, the best catfish, too. We got to have you two over for dinner soon."

We told her we'd love to come over.

"There are so many stories here," said Normagene. "There wasn't a board put into this house that my daddy didn't nail."

Bill said quietly that he put the upstairs bathroom in himself.

"Come on now," Normagene said. "You had some help."

"OK," said Bill. "I had some help."

Before they left, Normagene pointed to the magnolia, which had begun to blossom light pink flowers. "In my entire life, this tree opened up only a few times. Now look at it. It's blooming this year."

It did again the year after that, and the year after that, and the year after that; it bloomed until we moved out.

The First Invasion

I slept on the futon upstairs; I often did when it got too late to drive back home. I didn't sleep well. Gusts of wind always blew the branches of the tree outside against the window; it sounded like fingers tapping on the glass. Katie kept a plant light on downstairs; the light cast an eerie nocturnal glow throughout the night, which made strange wavering shadows in the evergreen and the prairie grass. I wasn't used to the sounds of the house: the scurry of tiny feet, the drone of something electrical, the creaky roof rafters.

In the dark, I could be melodramatic.

It wasn't only the night that kept me awake. It was my mind.

Katie was downstairs, right below me. I listened hard for her breath. Sometimes, the dogs shifted in their sleep, their collars jingling. Sometimes, Katie snored. And twice, she got up to use the bathroom.

Not long after the magnolia bloomed, Katie admitted there was something more than friendship between us. We remained cautious, however, afraid of ruining a friendship. We found that when we didn't want to talk about us, we talked about the house.

"I think we should repaint the walls," I said.

"What color?"

"Just a fresh coat of white."

"All the walls?"

"The bathroom and your bedroom."

"Sounds good," Katie said. "How about an area rug for the upstairs?"

"It could cover up some holes."

"Do you think we need more flowers?"

"Of course. I love those snapdragons."

The night had begun to lighten, the birds stirring in the trees. I didn't know what time it was when I heard someone coming up the stairs. The steps creaked. I closed my eyes and pretended to be asleep. A body slid next to mine. A hand fell on my hip. A head buried into my neck.

"There was this bug." A whisper. "I got scared."

"It's OK," I said. "Go to sleep."

"It was big," she said, "and . . ." Before she could finish the sentence she drifted off.

☙

A few days later, Katie asked Bill: "I'm thinking about asking Ira to move in with me. I just wanted to know whether you'd be comfortable with that arrangement."

"If he's OK with you," Bill said, "then he's OK with us."

The Other Tenants

A year later and Katie and I never did anything to the inside of the house. We did not patch up the crack that was getting larger and larger in the bedroom. We never painted any of the rooms as we planned. All that was different about the house was our stuff. Our couch. Our satellite TV. Our computers. Our pictures. Our bed. Us. The farmhouse remained the same, and we were just as happy.

Katie figured the farmhouse existed in another dimension. She was an avid reader of science fiction and fantasy novels, and she felt the farmhouse was in a timeless place. When we passed those two hickories, we were cut off from the rest of the world, and all the rules that governed that world did not apply here. Because of this, the house resisted change; maybe even resented it.

It wasn't just the house. It was the land. Katie and I had big plans for a garden. We dug around trees, planted annuals, pulled weeds, and mulched to prevent more weeds from growing back. Despite our best efforts, our garden was quickly taken over, our flowers choked out in a couple of days. Our roses developed a strange disease that ate away at the leaves, and left the bushes bare; our peonies never opened during the four years we were there. Blackberry bushes took over our yard, their thorns snagging the dogs. One afternoon, I cut every blackberry bush down—every one I could find— but the next day, another one would just grow in its place; another one would prick my skin; another one would snag the dogs.

"Sometimes I feel like I'm not me," Katie said. We were outside planting, trying hard to make something happen.

"Like being possessed?" I had found an old rusted cylinder that must have been part of a tractor. It weighed fifty pounds, and I stood it up near the sad state of our roses, facing south into the fields. We were going to plant a moon vine at the base of the cylinder and put a pot of pansies on top of it.

"Not quite. Like what I'm doing and thinking is what she was doing and thinking."

"Who is this she?"

"The farm wife."

"What farm wife?"

"Normagene's mother. I feel like I understand her. Or we understand each other."

"How can you understand someone you've never met?"

"I think we are the same people sometimes." Katie went on to say that she felt most like the farm wife when she was outdoors, in the evening, and at times, she felt as if she were being led into the fields, walking in the same steps, discovering the same things—the clean bones of an animal, the skin of a snake, a powder-blue cornflower. "Sometimes, I feel like she tells me to hang more bird feeders. She loves birds."

"Maybe you're her reincarnated soul," I said. I was Buddhist. I was constantly on the lookout for my past lives.

"Maybe," she said. "I get this feeling, though, besides the feeders, she doesn't want anything to change here."

☙

But we were changing. Day by day, we were learning more about each other. We were beginning to look beyond our current lives on McDaniel Drive, looking further into the future, and that future didn't involve this house, this place we had grown so familiar with, this place we loved. Our future was elsewhere.

In the year I lived there, however, I had given myself over to Katie and the farmhouse. I started understanding what it was that attracted her to it in the first place, started to even feel the farm wife in me. It was not a ghostly possession, but a sense of calm, like the act of a deep appreciative sigh, that tiny exhale of air that lifts the weight of the world off your chest. It might have been the farm wife's eyes I was looking through, when on some days, the sky seemed so large that I imagined instant flight. Or her lips I used to whistle at the sparrows high in the trees. Or her hands that hung our laundry on the line.

I trusted this place.

In the morning, when I let the dogs out for their morning pee, I sometimes emerged out the backdoor naked, standing without thought of who would see me, knowing no one would.

∽

That was when they began to show themselves, the other tenants.

A wren nested in the front porch. We entered and exited the house through the back door, so we wouldn't disrupt it during its nesting period . . . And then there was the mouse that found its way into the bag of jasmine rice. It was gray and stealthy, and always managed to make me squeak with its sudden movements . . . And the muskrat that was chomping down on purple clover outside the dining room window. It lived by the old septic pond . . . And there was the king snake that coiled around the thickest branch of the tree closest to our bedroom window . . . And there was the groundhog that lived under the propane tank . . . And there was the possum in the attic, whose tail I saw once, hanging through a crack in the ceiling . . . And the tiny tree frogs that suction-cupped our windows . . .

We were never alone. Most of the time, we lived together in peace.

The Fall

A windstorm whipped through southern Illinois. The tornado sirens went off, and I kept looking at the darkened green sky for a funnel cloud. Thunder shook the ground. Wind slammed the house. Rain pelted the roof. The farmhouse screamed and moaned. Every creak, every rattle was amplified.

The dogs stuck close to me, perking their ears up at all the noise. Nothing calmed them, not my voice, not my offers of treats, not my loving pats. At one point, I thought the entire house would topple over.

Through all of this, Katie napped in the bedroom, her snores joining the cacophony of sounds.

Then there was an earthquake, or it felt like an earthquake. It lasted three seconds. Some of the pictures on the wall went crooked. The leaves of the houseplants quivered. The crashing sound quieted everything, the period after the last sentence of a book.

Soon after, the sun peeked through the widening spaces in the clouds, and the cardinals and chickadees came back to their perches on the trees.

Katie woke up. She looked groggy; lines from her pillowcase indented her cheeks. "I had a strange dream."

"I can't believe you slept through that," I said, the dogs resting on either side of me, finally at ease.

"Through what?"

"I think you should look outside."

Katie went to the laundry room window. I followed. She tilted her head. "Wow."

"Yeah."

About a foot from the house was the largest tree in the yard. It had uprooted itself and fallen over. Some of the branches pushed up against the house. The tree took down the phone line. It crushed some of the daffodils and tulips we had planted in the front entrance.

Normagene once told me the many trees around the farmhouse were as tall now as they were when she was a child. That was what her Mama loved about the house. The shade. It protected the house from the penetrating summer heat. But it never impeded the view, only framed it, like a painting. When the tree stood, I had often marveled at the thickness of it. When I looked up, there seemed no end to the tree; I could never see the top. I had the feeling that if I began climbing it, the branches and limbs would take me to secret places.

"We should probably call Bill," I said.

"I guess so," said Katie. Her eyes did not leave the tree. "If it had fallen ten feet more to the left . . ."

" . . . you would've been crushed," I said. "And ten feet to the right . . ."

". . . it would've landed on the propane tank and we would've exploded."

"We should probably call Bill," I said.

"Yeah."

We didn't leave the window, though. We kept staring at the tree. On the ground it didn't seem that big anymore. It looked small, in fact, a fraction of what it used to be. Squirrels scurried along the truck, horizontally. A downy woodpecker landed on it and pecked. Where the tree had uprooted itself, the ground appeared as if a tiny meteor had crashed into the earth.

"You said you had a strange dream," I said.

"I don't remember it anymore."

☙

Perhaps it was the tree that began the invasion. Perhaps, in its quake, it shifted the balance of the natural world.

Six months after the tree fell, I asked Katie to marry me on a ski lift in Colorado, and not long after that I was offered a job in upstate New York. Katie and I agreed to move there by the end of summer, giving us a year to pack and ready ourselves for the next part of our lives.

What we weren't ready for were the hornets that entered the house and flew around the light in our bedroom. They were as thick as thumbs, and they scared us. At times there were eight to ten of them. They barely made a sound. We called an exterminator, but when he arrived, there were no hornets to be seen. He checked around the light fixture and told us he did not know where they were coming in from. There were no traces of them at all.

The hornets never appeared in the daylight, but as soon as night fell, there they were, flying around our bedroom light.

The dogs sensed how scared we were and went about the house with their tails low, their ears back—Bonny, especially; she was always attuned to our moods. We went about disposing of the hornets with a tennis racket and my 12-inch shoe. I swatted them out of the air and Katie smashed them wherever they landed.

Once, after visiting Katie's family in Champaign for a couple of days, we came back to a bedroom filled with hornets.

"I'm scared," Katie said.

"Let's get out of here," I said. "Bring the dogs."

We headed into town and rented a room at the Super 8 motel.

"We need a room for one night," I said.

"We got mutant bees," Katie said.

The hotel clerk smiled, but said nothing.

The next morning, when we went back, we expected to see hundreds of them flying in the house. We expected the farmhouse to be one big hive. But there were none. No evidence that they were even there.

We stopped by at Bill and Normagene's to tell them about the hornets. They lived only a field away.

"Oh, poor Bill got stung by one," said Normagene.

Bill took out a little container with a hornet in it. He shook it around. The hornet floated in fluid. "We took it in to the lab at the university. They said these guys are from Brazil. Said they're pretty rare."

"And mean, too," Normagene said. "Bill, honey, what did it feel like when you got stung?"

"Like someone shot me in the back," he said. "Knocked the wind clear out of me."

"I'm afraid for the dogs," Katie said.

"Understandable," said Normagene. "I couldn't imagine if one of my babies got stung." The Warners had two scrappy Scottish terriers.

"You say you don't know how they're getting in?" Bill said.

"We checked everywhere," I said.

"They like the light," Katie said.

"Turn them off then," Normagene said.

For the next couple of months, we lived in the dark.

The End

The squirrels. They scratched the walls the entire summer, waking us up at six. Once, I hit the walls a few times, and all we heard was a moment of quiet before the scratching started again.

By then, we were ready to move on.

In that year, our lives would change. We would lose Mick to a brain tumor, and then Bonny a year later. We would buy our first home in Oswego, New York, a 1984 Lincoln Log cabin. We would get married twice, in Thailand for my family and Illinois for Katie's. We would uproot ourselves and leave Illinois, the state we were born and raised in. Our lives in the farmhouse had come to an end.

Minus the tree, the farmhouse and its property hadn't changed. Even where the tree had fallen, another was growing in its place. On one of our last days together, Katie and I flew a kite in the middle of the field. I had never flown a kite before. It was a cheap thing we bought in town with bright colors and ribbon streamers. Katie told me to run with it and then let it go. My first few attempts, the kite dragged on the ground.

"You have to trust the wind," she said.

I tried again. I ran as fast as I could and released the kite. The wind caught the kite this time and it lifted it up in the air. I let the spool of string unwind slowly, the kite rising higher and higher.

Katie and I spent our first four years together at the farmhouse, and where the kite flew was the only vantage we had not seen the house from. What did we look like from the sky, I wonder, what did the land look like?

Katie and I often reminisce about the McDaniel house. Bill and Normagene sent us letters during the holiday season. They were getting older. The upkeep was getting harder for Bill. In one of letters, Normagene wrote: *You two were our best tenants. No one else loved the house as much as you did.*

Katie said once, "Even if we didn't move, the land was reclaiming the house. There was nothing anyone could do."

"What about the farm wife?"

"Even she couldn't stop it."

And it seemed only right, that after nearly a century, the house was returning to a time before it was a house, a time before any of us happened onto it, and it was taking with it sediments of stories, layers of memory.

The farm wife knew this. She knew it was time to leave. The farm wife walked into the golden field, her birds flying overhead, and with one last look at her house, she disappeared into the land.

Into the Country

I am at two with nature.

–Woody Allen

When I first met my wife, I pretended to be a hiker.

"I love the outdoors," I said. "The trees, the wind. Exhilarating." On our first hike, a mile and a half up a mountain (small hill) that scraped along the edges of a steep (gentle) cliff, she blazed on ahead of me while I tried not to hyperventilate each time I looked down.

"You're not a nature guy, are you?" she asked after the hike.

We sat on a bench at the trailhead. My knees ached. I sweated in places that shouldn't. I took off my Doc Marten boots to check the forming bubbles on the soles of my feet. I ate flies and mosquitoes by the dozen every time I opened my mouth to breathe. "What do you mean? This is fantastic."

There was nothing out of sorts about Katie's appearance. Her brown hair remained perfectly held in by a clip, not a single straying strand. She breathed like a Buddhist monk, quiet and even, and appeared as if she could walk the trail again, walk it forever. "You can tell me the truth," she said. "You suck." She giggled into her oversized sleeve. She looked good in my sweatshirt.

Katie was right. In nature, I did suck. I'm not made for the outdoors. When spring comes around, you'll be able to find me by following the trail of Kleenex, listen to my booming sneezes and trumpet nose. I'm allergic to everything. Name it and I'll sneeze. In the sun, I wilt. Red bumps spread across my back and neck. My scalp dries and flakes. I look as if I have been crying for days, my eyes like soft cherries. Most of the time, I'm scratching some part of my body, complaining about the heat, about the swarm of gnats crowning my head. I'm Happy Hour for mosquitoes, their favorite Thai cocktail.

I'm about the city. Born in Chicago. Raised in a suburb. Nature lover in the comfort of an air-conditioned room, museum, indoor arboretum. Hiking and camping via eco-documentaries. I was a Boy Scout and sucked at it. Still, I get breathless at a hovering hummingbird, a golden rain, the sunset over Lake Ontario, a tornado in the Kansas plains.

Katie, however, seemed to sprout from the earth itself. We have often talked about our family vacations. When she reminisces about hers, she speaks of the high peaks of Wyoming and Colorado, the wildflowers growing along deep sunny slopes. She speaks of fishing trips and swims in isolated Canadian lakes, of riding in an RV and once escaping a forest fire. She has deep, deep sighs of appreciation for the outdoors. Listening to her is like watching *NOVA* on PBS. In her stories, birds chirp. Horses kick up dust. In her stories, streams trickle along rocky bottoms and waterfalls thunder below. Her tales are never marked by her age, but by landmarks and animals and memorable trails and even more memorable adventures.

My vacations weren't into nature, but America's gaudy tourist hotspots: Wisconsin Dells; Disney World; Niagara Falls; Branson, Missouri. My family loved going to Brookfield Zoo—our special nature excursions—balloons tied around my wrists, my hands stained by a melting Good Humor bar, a stuffed monkey wrapped around my neck. My vacations come back to me in neon signs and electronic buzzes. I remember gift shops that sold T-shirts, hats, buttons, water globes, fake Indian moccasins, postcards and calendars. I remember playing countless rounds of miniature golf, the Tommy Bartlett's Ski and Sky Show, Sea World's dancing dolphins. While Katie's family surrounded themselves with trees, we surrounded ourselves with people and traffic and noise, lots and lots of mechanical noise.

One year, instead of staying at the Shamrock Motel on the main strip in the Wisconsin Dells, my father suggested we camp.

"Like in a tent?" I asked. I was seven and the prospect of sleeping in a tent sounded both adventurous and scary.

"Yes," said my father. "Camping." He said the word like it was something strange and exotic.

My father bought a six-person tent for three people and gathered outdoor supplies: an axe, aluminum cooking utensils and plates, flashlights, a mallet, three heavy-duty winter sleeping bags (even though we were going to camp in the heat of July), and a Swiss Army knife. Looking at the supplies, I thought of the Himalayas. I thought of chopping down towering trees. I thought of the men I saw on TV with long, rugged beards, who only wore flannel. I imagined the wilderness, my wilderness, which was wild and fantastic, a combination of everything I had seen when watching nature shows and everything my imagination dreamt up.

When my father pulled into Yogi Bear's Jellystone Campground—touted as winning the Excellence and Pinnacle Award since 1976—my impression of our nature trip was slightly skewed. The campground was crowded with white people, most of them rowdy, loud little kids. At Jellystone, there was a miniature golf course, an enormous pool with waterslide, an arcade room, and hourly "Hey" rides. As we made our way through the campground, we passed men watching portable TVs outside their tents, women cooking on portable grills instead of campfires, siblings chasing, kicking, and stabbing each other with twigs. We found our lot and pulled our Oldsmobile station wagon in between two RV's. Quietly, my mother and father set up the tent, fumbling with yellow stakes and light aluminum poles. I read the directions out loud, sitting on our lot's picnic table. But I was distracted. A blonde boy, about five years old, stood ten feet away, staring at us. Perhaps a family of Thais trying to put up a tent was a spectacle to him, a rare and wondrous sight, like the Aurora Borealis or a full rainbow.

After thirty minutes, the tent was up. We crawled in and sat in the glow of red canvas. The tent cut us off from the world outside, dulled the noise, dulled everything. At motels, there was always the TV to distract us. Part of the appeal of going to motels was the free HBO and other cable channels, and during down times, we flipped on the TV and zoobed out. In the tent, we stared at each other, not sure of our next step. My father cleared his throat a few times, and my mother and I straightened up, thinking my father was going to give us his itinerary of fun. Instead, he played with his chin. After ten minutes in the tent, I felt like a cookie baking in an oven.

"I want to go to a motel," I said.

My mother told me to shush, and I did, and we continued to sit in silence.

After another ten minutes, I said, "I want to go to a motel."

My mother looked at my father. My father shrugged, and then, wordlessly, we exited the tent, emerged into the bright July sun. My mother and father started taking everything down, reloading the car, and the blonde boy was still there, staring.

☙

Bangkok, "Village of Wild Plums," has become a metropolis. What used to be a kingdom of canals is now packed with busses, taxis, motorcycles, and automobiles. The city bristles with consumerism. McDonald's, Starbucks, KFC dot city streets. And the malls: Robinson, Central, Siam Square with stores like DKNY, Armani, Versace. Strip clubs advertise in bright lights. Corporations are housed in high-rises. New ten-story condominiums pop up like lilies. Eight-lane highways bisect and branch into other eight-lane highways that bisect and branch into others. The city spreads.

Still, despite technological advances, eighty percent of Thailand's sixty million people still reside in rural areas, and most of that eighty percent work in agriculture. Comparatively, seventy-seven percent of the United States population lives in cities or suburbs.

Imagine then the poor boy who lives in a shack next to a marshy rice field. For him and many who live in rural villages, the opportunity to get to the city may never come. If he is fortunate enough, he may find a job in Bangkok, become a rare success story, a legend. *The one who went away*, the villagers might say. *The one who now drives a BMW.* The boy will become a story of possibility. And once he is in the city, carried away by the traffic, the hustle and bustle, the quickened pace of life, he won't look back. Not at the shack or the rice field.

In the states, I often hear: "I need to get away from it all. I'm going into the country." In Thailand, no one says such a thing. *Why*, they'd wonder, *go to the country when we are already there? Why go into the country when we are looking to get out?*

A few years back, we drive through the lush green of central Thailand, my mother pointing out the places of her childhood. The land stretches out like a midwestern prairie. The area where my mother lived as a child is green, and anything green is wild. Sparrows dart across the land; gangs of dogs roll in the dusty roads; and the sounds are not of car horns or the buzz of electricity that permeate the world I have become accustomed to, but of a natural quiet, of the wind through trees and grass, the speedy ticking steps of a tiny creature, and the trill of geckos.

As my mother points to various things outside our air-conditioned car, in my imagination, she begins to take a different shape. Suddenly, she is not just a mother who lives in Oak Lawn, Illinois. She is not a mother at all, but a girl who paddles a canoe to school, who runs her hand along the rough sides of elephants, who dives off bridges and swims among the snakes and piranhas.

The car cuts through the land and she simply points at what is outside in the humidity and hot air that steams up our windows. She offers nothing more. No explanation. No story. *There*, she points. *And there.* We travel at 80 kph and her youth flies by in a blur before I can make sense of it. That is what my mother thinks of her prior life. A blur of green. A fleeting, distant buzz. I wonder, in that stretching and yawning land, whether those who come from a world like this will want to return to it. I wonder whether the reason my mother does not tell me her stories is because she does not see the beauty in the landscape. Instead, nature to my mother equals poverty. Equals hardship. Equals regret. All of which are not beautiful, are not worth spending her breath on. And maybe, as her finger darts from one landmark to another, she is actually pointing beyond the tin-roofed houses, the brown creeks, beyond the flowering trees and lilies and lotuses outside the car window, beyond an ocean and mountains and countries. Perhaps what she is really pointing at is her new home, Chicago. Perhaps what she sees is something other than green, and what she hears is something other than the twittering birds and the howling dogs. Because, in the end, nature could not provide what she has now or who she has become: a nurse, a homeowner, a mother with a family that means more to her than trees, creeks, and dragonflies.

❧

Two weeks before I start my fourth of five years at Southern Illinois University Carbondale, a few months before I meet Katie, my mother and I decide to spend quality time together, something we haven't done since my parents divorced. I buy a book entitled, *Enjoy Southern Illinois: A Complete Recreational Guide*, and I comb through the book for scenic places to take my mother. We decide not to spend our time secluded in my tiny apartment across the street from department stores like Famous Barr and K's Merchandise. Instead, we venture out and explore. For the first week, we drive through the Shawnee National Forest, spanning the bottom tip of Illinois. We visit Garden of the Gods, ranked tenth in the United States for sandstone rock formations, and the Little Grand Canyon in Murphysboro, a four-mile steep trek in a deep ravine filled with ferns and frogs.

On the seventh day, we drive to LaRue/Pine Hills Ecological Area. Unlike the other days of sun, billowy cumulous clouds darken the sky and the tree cover is so thick it makes me feel closed in, trapped. My mother seems out of sorts, too, more jumpy. Every snapping twig, every cackle from the crows puts her in a state of restlessness and unease. Her eyes are wide, darting from sound to sound, as if expecting someone or something to jump out and abduct us. We say very little during the day besides "pretty" or "beautiful" or comments about the weather. The guidebook says we should hike Inspiration Point trail, which leads to Inspiration Point, a phallic limestone rock formation. On the tip of the point, the books says, one can see the Big Muddy River, the Illinois plains to the north, the Shawnee National Forest spreading east and west.

A few steps before we reach the point, my mother insists we turn back.

"*Ta mie?*" I ask. Why?

"Not feel good." She is pale, her cheeks flushed.

"We're almost there, though."

"Please," she says. A slithering garter snake startles her.

"Whatever," I say and turn around.

As we round the corner at the trailhead, a white Nissan pickup truck with orange flames on the car door zooms off. When we get into the car, my mother says, "Purse gone."

"What?"

"Purse," she says. "Gone."

"Are you sure?" I get out of the car, open the back, and rummage through empty water bottles, old magazines, books, and dirty sweaters. Nothing.

I hop back into the driver seat, start the car and squeal out, going sixty along the curvy, forested road. My mother holds on to the dash. She tells me to slow down. I don't listen. I chew on my lip. The car skids on some rocks, goes over a few potholes and puddles. Still, no pickup in sight. Instead, there are five men in camouflage walking along the side of the road. Their faces are painted black and green. All of them have rifles slung over their shoulders. Some wear hats, and the ones that don't have short buzz cuts.

I stop beside them and roll down the window. My mother has her hand on the car locks. She pins herself against her door.

"Did you see a white pickup?" I ask them. "Did one just speed by here?"

The men stare. One chews on a blade of grass. One wipes his nose with the back of his hand. One spits.

"A white pick up with flames," I say louder. I talk like sales clerks who try to help my mother in department stores. Slow. Over-enunciating. "Did you see one?"

No one answers. They look back and forth among each other. Then one of them shrugs and says, "We seen nothing."

There is only one road out of LaRue, the road I am on.

An hour later, at the police station in Anna, my mother tells the officer what was in the purse. He jots everything down in a black notebook. Six hundred dollars cash. Credit cards. Receipts. Driver's license. Pocket packs of Kleenex. Gum. Vapor rub. Tiger Balm. A gold Buddha pendant she's had since she was ten valued at well over a thousand dollars, but priceless in sentiment. I translate for my mother who resorts to Thai, her safe language. She speaks like someone is sitting on her chest, soft with heavy-weighted words. The phrase she repeats is *mie me cone*. No people. There were no people at LaRue. At other places we passed smiling faces, couples walking their dogs, anxious students like me waiting for the semester to start. There was a cornucopia of cars in the parking lot. We were among many. We weren't alone. At LaRue, however, there were no other signs of life besides the natural life, flora and fauna. We were out in nowhere. We were strangers, and that feeling of displacement seemed to hover and cast a dark shadow over us.

After taking down our story and inspecting the car, which has no marks of a break-in, the officer shakes his head. "That's a wild place over there," he says. "For you folks, it's not the safest place to ever be."

❧

In the spring of 1998, Katie rented an old farmhouse on the outskirts of Carbondale, far from strip malls and college-town traffic. As our relationship grew intimate, I spent more and more time there. The house had a lot of character—wide French doors, tall ceilings, an upstairs reading nook that overlooked the backyard. But it, alone, did not captivate Katie's attention. Around the farmhouse was land that seemed to stretch on forever. Here was the Midwest as it was: a calming sea of earth. When I arrived at the house, I often caught Katie staring out and breathing deeply.

In *The Flatness and Other Landscapes*, Michael Martone writes: "This landscape can never take us emotionally in the way smoky crags or crawling oceans can. We stare back at it. Beneath our skins, we begin to disassemble the mechanisms of how we feel. We begin to feel." For years, I drove as fast as I could through the flattest parts of Illinois and said, "This is the most boring looking state ever." But spending time in such openness, I realized there were things I never understood about the nature of landscape, even more, about myself. I wanted to see what Katie saw, wanted that love and appreciation of the natural world. What I discovered, at first, was how vulnerable I felt, how exposed the openness made me feel. Once we walked into the fields, and I had the sudden urge to flee back into the house. This urge came on when I realized I was in the middle of nothing, and when I looked in all directions, all I saw was land and sky. I imagined at any moment I would be flattened. By what?—I did not know.

When I stayed the night at Katie's, I rarely slept, listening to the aches and moans of the house, listening to the coyotes at night. During the day, I jumped at the sudden movement of birds and bats in the old chicken houses, now used for storage, jumped at the frogs that leapt away from my lumbering steps. I was not afraid of birds, bats, or frogs; I was afraid of the possibility of the unknown; nature was an uncontrollable question mark.

"You're such a city boy," Katie said to me one day.

I couldn't deny it. "Don't you get scared out here?"

"Of what?" she said, her right eyebrow rising. "What's there to be afraid of?"

I didn't know.

Katie went on to tell me how the farmhouse, the land, reminded her of her childhood, and when she looked out into the fields she was seeing her past. She trusted the landscape, the one thing in her life she knew would not wrong her, an ever-present faithful friend. I didn't allow that trust in my life—none of my family did. We were continually looking for the next obstacle, the next sudden movement that would throw our lives out of balance. Moreover, we were visitors in this country. We did not own any part of it. We were displaced. We felt lost.

But I found Katie, and with her, I discovered another world. The more time I spent at the farmhouse, the less afraid I became. I began to admire the birds at the feeders, instead of fearing that one would fly into the house and cling to the curtains. I learned the names of flowers and trees, learned to decipher the sounds of nature. I saw the land differently, not with the same longing as Katie—I don't think I will ever see the world quite the same as she—but I recognized in that wide-open space there was a place for me, a place for us, and this thought comforted me.

"The thing about flatness," Katie once said, "is you always see everything coming."

～

When I was diagnosed with diabetes, a friend suggested I take a break. Get out into nature. Take some time to breathe. He suggested a place to stay and relax with other people with similar interests. I spent three weeks with artists, activists, and writers in the heart of the Adirondacks. During my stay, I watched loons dive into the lake, heard their nightly screams. Once, during dinner, a black bear cub and its mother lumbered onto the property, and we gathered at the window in awe. Daily, I experienced something new, which is the essence of being in nature; no two days are ever the same. I began to catalog my stay in a wire notebook. I listed the animals I encountered: a snapping turtle, a gray fox, a mink, flying squirrel, porcupine, woodchuck, beaver. And for the first week, the thrill of such discoveries made me venture out on some of the trails around the property.

After the first week, however, I began to yearn for civilization. I missed my television, my Playstation 2. I wanted a cheeseburger and fries. I wanted a thick milkshake that would surely send me into a diabetic coma. I wanted McDonald's, but knew the closest one was over two hours away. Without a car, I trekked into town, where I heard there was a diner that served some decent greasy fare and a TV that usually had a sporting event on of some sort.

On my walk, I had a rare sighting, the rarest during my time in the Adirondacks. I was walking on the side of a road and coming towards me was a black Audi Sport. In the car was a young Asian man with a long ponytail and sunglasses. I did a double take, making sure my eyes weren't playing tricks on me. And when I confirmed that my eyes weren't lying, all I could do was stare. The man did the same. He slowed down, and I wondered whether we were thinking the same thing. "Are you lost? Don't you realize you, we, are in the Adirondacks?" The sight of him was jarring, reminding me of where I was, and suddenly, I was filled with a sense of panic and fear. Besides us there was nothing around but trees and trees and more trees. And what if we were lost, who would come to search for us? I imagined the police showing our pictures around town, and the locals shrugging and saying they hadn't seen people like us in a while. It was an illogical fear, Katie would say, one she kept reiterating to me when we lived in the farmhouse, but it was fear nonetheless.

As the Audi was about to pass, I waved, and the man behind the wheel nodded and smiled, as if to say, "What up, my brother?" My eyes followed the car until it disappeared behind the bend and I was suddenly alone with the realization that the man in the car, my Asian brother, was heading *somewhere*, out of the woods.

I turned around. Retraced my steps until I found my way back where later that night I continued my list: a snapping turtle, a gray fox, a mink, flying squirrel, porcupine, woodchuck, beaver, Asian man in Audi . . .

જી

One of my mother's last vacations before she moved back to Thailand was to Maine. She was making a northeast swing. In the last year, she made it a point to fly to Hawaii, and then two weeks later, she drove to Alaska with some friends. She wanted to see every last bit of the country before she left. She wanted to see the Maine coastline and eat pounds and pounds of lobster with a plastic bib tied around her neck.

Katie and I packed the car and rented a cheap motel room for four days. We stayed in the Acadia National Park area. In the morning and afternoon, we hiked a few trails, but not as many as my wife would've liked. We went on a whale watching tour where my mother and I suffered from severe seasickness, our faces in puke bags. Katie, on the other hand, stood outside on the deck, the wind blowing through her hair as she pointed and smiled at sea ducks and terns and the rare puffin that circled our boat. In the evening, we ate at gaudy restaurants and capped the night off with a round of miniature golf at Pirate's Cove.

Near the end of our trip, on one of our driving excursions, I pulled the car over to look at eider ducks clustered on a rock sticking out of the ocean. Katie whipped out her binoculars. My mother whipped hers out, purchased with Katie's advice expressly for the trip, and I stood there zooming in with my digital camera. The thing I learned about nature, the thing I learned from being around Katie's family, is nature is not about the obvious. Nature is about the small. It is about the little things that move us.

Off to the right, a bird sang. A soft delicate sound. My mother heard it first and cocked her ears toward the song.

"I hear it too," Katie said.

I heard nothing but the lapping ocean waves.

The two of them took off into the woods, my mother's small body leading the way.

"Beautiful sound," my mother said, staring from one branch to another.

Katie nodded silently.

Their eyes went from limb to limb, scanning the trees, the evergreens, the brush on the ground. They turned at the slightest sound—a peep, a flutter of wings.

After a few minutes of searching, my mother said, "There," and pointed to a thicket of branches.

I saw nothing.

Katie flashed her binoculars where my mother pointed. "I think it's a warbler. A black and white warbler."

"So pretty," said my mother.

"Yes it is." Katie kept as still as possible.

Both of them stood there, watching the bird, remarking on its coloring, its size.

Later, back in the car, Katie said, "Chin, you have wonderful eyes, a born bird watcher."

"I liking them all," my mother said, her eyes pointed toward the ocean for more discoveries.

Though I never saw the black and white warbler, did not even hear its song, in that moment was a different kind of sighting of a different kind of bird, one that sang a song that bridged two families and two cultures.

Once, driving back from a golf course in Crowne Point, Indiana, I noticed something running beside the car. I was nine and bored of the long drive home and hungry after eighteen holes of swinging the stick. I leaned my forehead against the car window. The something skirted through the tall grass along the side of the road. It was a bird. Like a turkey. No.

Turkeys were ugly. This was majestic. More like the peacocks in Thailand. The head was dark green, iridescent. When it ran through shadow and light, its head turned from blue to purple to black to green again. Red circled the eyes, and there was a bright white ring around its neck. Its back feathers were spotted brown and white and yellow with a bit of orange. The bird kept up with the car, kept up at thirty miles an hour, until it decide to duck to the right and into a field of tall grass that looked like gold because of the setting sun.

The bird was a pheasant, I found out later. But what struck me was I didn't tell my father, who was driving. I didn't shout out like my wife often does when she's with her family at hawks on electric poles or migrating ducks on rivers. I knew, even then, that a pheasant would evoke nothing but a glance and a half-hearted word of appreciation and that was it. Forgotten.

As the pheasant ran off into the field, into the back of my memory, my father asked right after the moment whether I wanted KFC for dinner, and I responded absolutely. In that instant, I had forgotten about the bird, forgotten about how cool it looked, how I craned my neck to absorb all the patterns in its tail feathers. Instead, I told my father I wanted extra mashed potatoes with extra gravy. I told him I wanted drumsticks only.

Katie's family would never forget. The sighting of the pheasant would be cataloged with other rare sightings. The sighting of the pheasant would lead to discussions of other birds, other trips, other nature things. It would lead to other memories. And since marrying her, I've inherited this, too, this sharing of the natural world. *Do you remember the warbler in Maine? The storks in Bangkok? The wild turkey in the blizzard?*

Yes, of course, they—even the warbler I did not see—were beautiful.

To Kill a Thought: A Confession

The bullet is already in the brain; it won't be outrun forever, or charmed to a halt.

–Tobias Wolff, "Bullet in the Brain"

What happens first is you lose your vocabulary. You can't for the life of you describe what you feel because what you feel is akin to a tornado that has devoured a barn; there is just too much debris whirling around, disorienting and dangerous. This, for a lover of words, is a distressing truth and the first sign that something is wrong. You know this. You comprehend the word "wrong," linguistically recognize the origins of it— Old Norse, *rangr*, meaning *awry*. "Wrong" is the only descriptor you have, however, and it is not concrete. It is not what you preach to your students when you tell them they have to be precise with language, that they shouldn't tell you the cake was good, but to analyze the anatomy of the cake—the scattering of crumbs that cling, the icing that is slick and sweet on the tongue. Give me the lemon zest, you tell them. Give me the miniscule burst of vanilla beans, you say. Give me precision. But it is exactly precision you lack. So this is what happens: you sloth your day away on the couch, staring through the television, not realizing you, a thirty-three-year-old man, have been watching a *Dora the Explorer* marathon for the last three hours, and your ears, though they catch a Spanish word or two on the famed children's TV show—*frio, caliente*—have not processed a thing. You are in a state of turning, pondering this absentness in the brainhearthead, an absentness that is impossible to voice, that has now stolen too many hours of sleep, that has made your body grow out of proportion, that has implanted ideas and images one should never have. You think, Will this ever end? You think, How much longer can I take this? And you think, Not much.

છ

My Thai mother says depression is so American. (Depression, Middle English, *to press down*). According to her, depression is a failing of the spirit, and Americans have weak spirits. American spirits do not have mythological Gods in them, like the greatest of the great Siamese warriors. They are empty and without fight. She reminds me that this is why Thailand has never been colonized by any other country, that Thai people do not suffer from this thing called depression. She says one is only depressed because one overthinks. She tells me I should find a path that will lead me away from suffering. This is Buddha's way. But what is this path she talks about? Where is the path to someone who feels he is in thick, impenetrable woods, and the trees and their weighty leaves are suffocating any suggestion of light?

Overthinking, my mother would say.

This is from a woman who sat in front of the bay windows of our suburban house for thirty years, sewing and watching the outside world rush by, her unhappiness in this country leading her, like me, into herself. This is from a woman who would go through silent periods for weeks and walk the upstairs of the house like a zombie. This is from a woman who has mastered a different word: Repression.

છ

I read somewhere that the Dalai Lama said that people who speak the words "I," "Me," and "Mine" are more prone to become depressed. By this rationale, I—Me, Mine—am fucked.

છ

It is there, the two-ton elephant in the corner of the room, and the two-ton elephant is creeping up behind you, and the two-ton elephant has malicious plans. It wants to sit on your chest; it wants to drive you deep into the dirt; it wants to ground you into a pile of ashes. You can't hide from the two-ton elephant. You can't wish the two-ton elephant away.

In the past year, I've learned that we have a two-ton elephant lumbering around in our brains.

You do. Trust me.

The two-ton elephant lurks, waits. If you are fortunate, the two-ton elephant will remain sedate, or you will realize it isn't two-tons at all, but a miniature toy elephant that can fit in the palm of your spacious hand.

Here's the thing: I don't like to say the word depression.

I prefer two-ton elephant.

What comes with "depression" is a sense of vagueness, the dark under a blanket. I can see a two-ton elephant, the heavy weight of its ears, the rotund heft of its girth, the skinny rope of its tail, the elegant curve of its nose. I can even touch a two-ton elephant. Feel the mottled texture of its skin, the hot earth of its breath.

I understand that the two-ton elephant is a metaphor, and a metaphor by its very nature is a comparison, and a comparison is not an actuality. It is, as Susan Sontag suggests in *Illness as Metaphor*, an inadequate way to describe pain because it strips away genuine severity. And I understand that as a metaphor it could be whatever—an aardvark, a platypus, a naked mole rat—because metaphors can be made malleable; one can find something in anything. Still, when we try to describe our state of malaise, the first thing we do is jump into metaphor. "There is a black cloud in my brain," we say. "It feels like an ice pick is stabbing my retinas," we say.

In Winston Churchill's 1953 Nobel Prize speech, he referred to the darker periods in his life as the "black dog." Depression metaphors are endless. Though they do fail to describe the "true" state of our condition—language is not limitless after all—they become a comfort, something we can hold onto. It is like that Thai proverb about being ripped off: I'd rather hold poop than a fart. Translation: I'd rather have something than nothing. So, it's easier to touch a two-ton elephant, easier to register its weighty presence in your mind.

❧

A couple of years ago, a friend asked how I felt on a scale of one to ten, ten being "Fantasmigorical." It was early May, and we sat on his porch in Boise, the spring pushing out the first buds of the year. I hadn't seen my friend in a while, and I missed these moments of conversation on the porch, ones that delved deep below the surface, ones that could make me slightly uncomfortable (a good thing), one that made me lose track of time. He was a good friend, one of my best, and was prone to entering "the darkness," a term he used. When this happened I would not hear from him for months, years even. Once he disappeared for almost three years, emerging one day in my driveway, leaning against his white Honda, smoking, always smoking. When my friend vanishes, I do not ask him where he has been, or what he was doing during those times. I never chastised him for his absence, even though I missed him and felt the space he left in my life. Whenever he returned—this last time it was a short email that read "I'm back"—we would pick up where we left off, as if someone un-paused the movie of our friendship.

To answer his question, I told my friend it depended on the day.

"In general, though," he said. "What's your number?"

"In general," I said, "I'm good."

"That's not a number."

I looked at the laces of my shoes, noticed how uneven they were, how frayed, how any day now one of them might snap.

"I don't know," I said.

My friend took a drag from his cigarette and leaned back on the lawn chair. "I'm trying to simplify things," he said. "I wake up and ask myself what number I am today. The trick is you have to look yourself in the mirror."

"Why is that so important?"

"You see yourself say it. You see yourself admit something and what that looks like, and—I don't know—it makes it tangible."

I knew myself, knew that when I entered my own darkness, I was unwilling to look anyone, especially myself, in the eye. I knew that all I was really looking at was my brain and its flawed neurons and synapses, and I was wondering which one of the thousands was misfiring and not sending the right signals to whatever biological process that promoted happiness. And I thought about happiness and the lack thereof, and what it felt like, really felt like to be happy because I didn't remember anymore, and I thought of Buddha, his image, and his half open eyes and his half smile, and I thought that he too entered a darkness; it was the reason he ran into the woods to meditate and gain enlightenment. Suffering was darkness, suffering was depression, was the two-ton elephant, was the black dog.

"Right now," my friend said, "I'm a good eight. Solid."

"I don't know," I said.

"There's this thing about numbers," he said. "They go up. They go down."

I wanted to tell him my number had been the same for months now, to say I was tired, and the metaphorical hole I was in grew deeper and deeper, and, worse I didn't want to get out. I was growing comfortable within its confines, despite how little air there was.

"I'm about an eight, too," I said and forced a smile. "Here with you. Spring in the mountains. Eight."

"Solid," he said, but I knew he did not believe me.

એ

The icy finger, storm, deadening noise, absolute silence, the dark woods, the darkness, hell's black depths, abyss, black struggle, the ocean, sleepwalker, the edge, the spiraling staircase, the stuck elevator, the basement, the black struggle, beast, zombie, ghost, eclipse, prison, cave, hole . . .

એ

William Styron describes the effects of his depression thus: "It is a storm indeed, but a storm of murk. Soon evident are the slowed-down responses, near paralysis, psychic energy throttled back close to zero. Ultimately, the body is affected and feels sapped, drained." I read Styron's *Darkness Visible*, an account of his depression, over and over, trying to find some answer, because—this admission frightens me—because I was getting tired of myself.

Synonyms of tired: Sapped. Weary. Dogged.

This extended beyond the physical, and soon my mind could not focus. Or it could only focus on my malcontent, breaking it down only to find other layers, like the door behind a door behind a door. My life had become stalled.

Worn-out. Exhausted. Beat.

I caught myself once yawning for an hour straight. I yawned so much that I tore the right corner of my mouth. I couldn't stop. When I yawned, my eyes began to tear up, just slightly, and I shivered at the end of it. There was no reason for this fatigue. I just couldn't stop yawning.

"What's wrong?" Katie, said. "That's your one-thousandth yawn in the last ten minutes."

"Just tired," I said.

"You say that a lot lately."

"I'm tired a lot."

"Come take the dogs for a walk with me."

"Too tired."

"It will make you feel good."

"I doubt it."

"Tell me what's wrong."

"I'm OK," I said. "I'm just tired."

Bushed. Pooped. Spent.

❧

Ira: I'm not feeling too hot lately.
Buddha: Get better. For real.

Ira: Easy for you to say, oh great Enlightened One. Some of us don't have the luxury to run away, cut our hair, and meditate for years. We got these things called jobs.

Buddha: Don't be a dick.

Ira: I'm just saying, dude.

Buddha: Think happy thoughts then. Better yet, don't think at all.

Ira: You sound like my mom.

Buddha: She's close to Nirvana, you know.

Ira: Oh God.

Buddha: You mean, Oh me.

Ira: This isn't about you.

Buddha: That's the problem.

Ira: Listen, I've been reading your doctrine again, as confusing as it is, and I just don't get it. You teach us we have choices, and any one of them leads us in a different direction, right?

Buddha: The most important thing is you keep moving, leaving whatever ails you behind.

Ira: That's the problem. I feel like I've lost the power to choose. I look in every direction and what hovers over each path is a fog so thick that in the end I do nothing. I stand, rooted.

Buddha: Trees grow even when they are planted.

Ira: ?

Buddha: As long as you seek, you will be found.

Ira: What the hell does that mean?

Buddha: I thought you wanted *that* Buddha, you know, the one with fortune cookie logic.

Ira: No. I just want to stop hurting.

Buddha: I have a thought then.

Ira: Let's hear it.

Buddha: You won't like it.

Ira: Probably not.

Buddha: There's this thing called karma. You've heard of it?

Ira: Ah. Yeah.

Buddha: Maybe the reason you're suffering is because of all the shit you did in your last life. Maybe you were an ass, and now you are paying for all the assy things you did.

Ira: So I can't do anything about this?

Buddha: If you believe this theory.

Ira: Do you?

Buddha: This is not about me.

෴

Once, on the way to work, you were driving and nodding off at the wheel. Not nodding off like your eyes got heavy and then closed and the next thing you noticed you're wrapped around a tree. Not nodding off like that. You were driving, and it felt like you were looking *through* the world, as if through dappled glass. Your hands moved without command. The turning signal went on without thought. You noticed you were getting off I-75, but you weren't seeing the road or the other vehicles or the merge. It was simply as if you were outside your body, as if you had died and were looking through a shell, an entity without energy.

෴

It's my natural tendency to lessen the severity of the situation, to shrug it off like it was inconsequential. I am always saying things like, "It's nothing." "I'll be OK." "Don't worry about me."

But this was very consequential. This was not "nothing." I was *not* OK. Please worry about me.

For five, six, seven years, I suffered. (Latin, *suffere*, to bear). This amount of time seems short, considering the longevity of our lives. (See, what I did there? I tried to play it off. Tried to lessen what happened to me.) But when you have a two-ton elephant on your chest, time no longer registers in the same way. In fact, you lose all sense of linearity. For me, seconds moved backwards, moved years, moved months. I could not, as a Buddhists, live in the now. What was the now, anyway, but a hokey way of being? What was the now without the then? You see, time, for me, was like this paragraph: it started and it went in every which direction. I was living (a debatable word here) in so many disparate time zones, or better yet, because I was living entirely inside my head, time was irrelevant, and when time was irrelevant, who needed to be on time?

A famous psychiatrist line: "When did you start feeling this way?"

There is no start. Depression doesn't employ the *once upon a time* story structure. It does not move in chronological order because depression is the antithesis of order. It is suddenly there. Or perhaps, it has always been there.

℅

And here's the scariest part, and because I want to be frank about this, I will come out and say an even scarier word than depression: Suicide. I wanted to commit suicide. (Neo-Latin suicidium, *of one self*). Styron again: " . . . it is entirely natural that the victim begins to think ceaselessly of oblivion."

℅

Stop overthinking.
God, I'm so American.

℅

In the darkest times, I ruminated over a simple multiple-choice question.

If I had a gun, would I pull the trigger?
Yes.
No.

I thought about the simplicity of that action. I never thought about what would happen afterwards. I thought about the motion, the feel of the finger as it pulled back. I didn't think about the sound or the mess or what I would leave behind. I thought only about how the brain tells the body what to do, how pulling the trigger would be its last command, how it would take fractions of a second, mere fractions, to wipe away a life. I didn't think about anything else.

The last time this happened, in the middle of a Florida winter, I emerged from the gun-to-the-head imaginings and said, "Bang." I pulled the trigger. I watched myself do it. The grimace on my face, the pained expression right before the bullet entered the brain. I said, "Bang," loud enough to wake me. I said it the way I did in the high school play *Oliver* when the fake gun didn't go off, and it was my voice that killed the villain Bill Sykes. I said it, and as dark as this may sound, I was able to put the thought behind me. To function again. Pulling the trigger ended my suicidal thoughts. I shot myself and was not dead. I had killed a thought, and what happened was the bullet in the brain, the hole it created, let in a light I had not seen in a long while.

&

Buddha instructs us to follow every thought through. After all, he says, it is only a thought.

&

Here are more metaphors. Do with these what you will.

About eight years ago, a student wrote about her depression, while being depressed. She didn't know this. The most telling of her mistakes were the skips from past to present tense or moments when the point-of-view changed from first person to second. She relied on vague, generic statements. Except for one section, the one I remembered most, the one I clung to. She described a large moving truck making a wrong turn onto her dead end street and how she watched for long minutes as the driver tried to turn around. He'd back up and then move forward, back up, move forward. He wasn't making any progress, so she left the window, only to find the truck was gone an hour later.

I was five or six or seven and I took swimming lessons at Centennial Pool in a suburb of Chicago. The instructors were high school boys who insisted if we wanted to be real men, we had to jump off the high dive. The springboard bobbed me up and down. Beneath me was a blond-haired boy. He had acne dotting every inch of his face. Come on, he said. I'm scared, I said. Don't be a wuss, he said. I looked down again. All it takes is one step, he said. I shook my head. One step? I said. I'll be here, he said. Promise? I said. One step, he said. I took it.

Two years ago, I visited my in-laws in Illinois. In no other part of the world does the landscape bring forth such feelings of isolation. It is beautiful, however, in its loneliness. There, among the empty palette of land, stands a tree. Beyond that tree, a barn and silo, and further in the distance a country road with its dirt and bumps. My wife tells me we should travel slowly when the corn is high because you can't see what cars are coming; you can't see anything. Sometimes you can get lost and every direction looks the same. What do you do then? I asked her. Eventually, you'll find your way back, she said.

We ask ourselves, again and again, when does it end? We try hard to find a solution, something rational to explain our woe away. We dissect every inch of our psyche, because we believe, like a marathon, there is a finish line we cross, and miraculously, we are healed. We believe most illnesses have cures. If we have a cold, take vitamin C. If our finger is hurting, then stop touching the hot stove, dummy. We bitterly cling to a cause and effect model. But depression does not need cause, and depression *is* the effect itself. So where is an end when we can't locate the beginning? Where is the end when time does not register?

Styron was checked into the hospital the moment he could not kill himself. That night, his wife in bed, he listened to Brahms' *Alto Rhapsody*, and the music—at that very second—took a profound effect on him. " . . . and in a flood of swift recollection I thought of all the joys the house had known. . . . I realized I could not commit this desecration to myself." And it was this instant that time had meaning again, when suddenly months and days mattered, seconds and minutes and hours. For Styron, the realization that he could not commit suicide—though how many times, I wonder, had he died in his mind?—was the moment the clock started ticking. "For me the real healers were seclusion and time."

ల

You've never liked the mirror, never liked what you saw in its reflection. But today, you are determined. You hold your gaze. You notice there is more gray than black in your beard and hair. You notice the weighted sag under your eyes, the red circling the white. You look at your bare chest, the tattooed Buddha in the center of it, halo around his head glowing orange. He is nested in a jungle of chest hair. There are strange hairs on your shoulders, long curly things you want to yank out one-by-one, and that mole on your arm, the one you've had since birth, has slowly lost its color to the point you can barely see it. Interesting. And what about your uneven eyebrows and the little bumps on your forehead and freckles like your mother? When did this happen?

The truth: It happened when you weren't aware of time. When you were away for a bit, in the darkness, and you realized—really realized—you haven't looked at yourself in years. And now, here you are. Early morning, 6:42 am. Your shoulders and back, for the first time in a long while, are not hunched over. And look at that. Could that be a smile? You're feeling pleasant, actually, like waking from a good dream of a good kiss and the lingering effects of it are still on your lips. You look at yourself and say, "What are you today?" You look at yourself and say, "Give me a number."

Body Replies

*Our own physical body possesses a wisdom which we
who inhabit the body lack. We give it orders which
make no sense.*

–Henry Miller

Outside winter rages. Snow blinds. White out conditions.
The wind is a guttural animal against this old upstate building.
I swear I feel the sway of this place, feel the cold invading the
fissures of the structure. I know after this session I will have to
put on my heavy boots and double thick coat and enter the
storm. I know I will have to scrape and re-scrape the snow and
ice and slush off my car. And I know that every warm muscle I
have worked hard to stretch will shrink and tighten as soon as
I step foot outside. Yet, right now, I'm here. My three-hundred
seventy-pound Body, occupying this space that is free of judg-
ment, free of ridicule, free of self-loathing.

Mostly.

Peace pervades this yoga studio in Oswego, New York.
Incense permeates the space—fragrant and earthy. Candles
flicker on windowsill ledges, casting wavering light onto the
wooden floors. Buddha presides in the front of the rectangular
room. Over speakers is the sound of bells, like the ones tin-
kling on temples in Thailand.

Today, I am learning to walk.

We go from one end of the studio to the other, twelve of us
in varying speeds and strides. Our instructor, Howard, tells us
to feel the floor. "You are connected," he says.

I usually bristle at what sounds like new age instruction,
bristle at anything touchy-feely. Such sayings have struck me
as melodramatic and unnecessarily deep, bad fortune cookie
fortunes. But I let Howard's words sink in because I like How-

ard. I like his patience with me and Body, like his words of encouragement when I do positions Body is unaccustomed to. Plus, his gray beard is glorious.

I fixate on the word "connected." I try to merge Body and mind. I say, step. I say, walk. I say, gentle. The opposite happens. My feet slap the floor, startling my glassy-eyed neighbor, who flinches at the sound. The floor creaks and cracks. I am painfully aware of how clumsy Body is, and when that happens I turn on myself. I say, fat. I say, ugly. I say, stupid.

"Walking is difficult," Howard says. "We never think about it. We are always doing."

I take another step. Slow. Concentrate. Lift the foot. Place pad of foot on floor. Follow with heel. Shift weight forward. Again.

"This is how we were meant to walk," Howard says. "No shoes. No socks. Skin against earth. Feel it. Let that sensation spread from the bottom of your body to the top."

I lose my balance. I stagger. I sigh.

"It's OK, Ira," Howard says. He moves behind me. Watches my steps.

Sweat drips from my forehead.

"You're walking on the outside of your feet," Howard says. "Make sure the whole bottom touches. Even the little toe."

I'm conscious of my loud walking, of my audible breaths, thick and hot. The others are like stealthy ninjas, gliding over the surface of the floor, absent of thought, just doing.

"What are you thinking?" Howard says.

I don't tell him the truth. I don't tell him how much I hate myself, how much I hate Body. I don't tell him how much I hate that I can't walk correctly.

"I'm thinking heel then toe," I say.

Howard doesn't buy it. He tilts his head and puts a hand to his bearded chin. It is the look Santa might give when he's deciphering whether you've been naughty or nice. "It seems you are disconnecting. Am I right?"

I shrug, but he is. My mind and Body are not one. Have never been one. They are separate entities. I have disconnected from Body, allowed it to do what it wants, when it wants. I have lost control. I started yoga to get it back. To connect to it. But this exercise of walking—fucking walking—has depleted hope that this will ever happen.

"You can do it," Howard says. "Give it time."

Being large and diabetic, time is something I may have little of.

☙

Body as language: You are a fat run-on sentence that feeds like high schoolers on riblet day—no—hyenas at the feast—no—the famished and you are never sated never happy because you have long since forgotten what happiness feels like—real happiness—not the quick illusion of it every time you sit and eat because that happiness is temporary and what follows is a loathing that makes you want to pluck the hairs off your legs one at a time—no—scream until the throat bleeds—no—tear hunks of your meaty flesh and fling them off because when you eat you have forgotten the sensation of satisfaction the meaning of the word enough or plenty or sufficient or full because the word full suggests there is no more space no more room to justify one more bite of something that will cut your life by another year but the surprising thing is you find more room because there is always more to choke a heart to choke the veins to choke the arteries and still you can't help but feel that there are places in you that are empty and starving and you can't seem to feed them the right food can't seem to figure out this puzzle of hunger and you feel this endeavor is pointless like feeding goldfish pieces of goldfish—no—like a food critic at McDonald's—no—like a milk shake without the shake or the milk and these moments have become the saddest recognition of your life because it means you are powerless against what hurts you most which means you are powerless against your own self which means you can't stop what is sure to happen—who can?

At the yoga studio, my favorite time is the darkness at the end, after we have worked out every muscle, after we have sweated and strained. Howard turns off the lights and we get into our relaxed positions—lying supine, legs raised on a chair—and concentrate on breathing. His voice leads us into our relaxed states.

"Close your eyes," Howard says, "and release all your worries."

The darkness is a comfort. It is a body pillow I cling to. In the light, Body is front and center. In the dark, it disappears. It ceases to matter.

"Relax your shoulders, your neck, your back," Howard says. "Chase away that tension with your breath."

I spend most of my day trying to disappear. Trying to squash Body. I have, in many ways, created a perpetual darkness in my life. Many fat people do this. To hide ourselves, we exaggerate another part of our personalities. I put on a wide smile. I nod voraciously. I ask questions. I make people laugh. In this way, I place persona in front of Body. I make people see someone else entirely. This, perhaps, is why fat people have been stereotyped as jolly or good-natured, why fat people are expected to smile and tell a joke. What people forget, however, is this is a mask. We deny ourselves true feeling; we belittle our suffering. What people forget is that it takes a lot of energy to wear this mask day in and day out. Yet, at the same time, we live in the darkness because we fear what would happen when we let the light in. We fear what we might discover. Worse yet, what others might discover.

"Imagine your stresses as paper," Howard says. "Crumple them up. Throw them away."

Darkness hides our flaws—yes—but it hides us, too. It is the reason the boys in my neighborhood loved playing Hide-n-Seek at night. Darkness provided extra cover. Darkness provided shadows. If you wore black, you could disappear entirely. One of us would never be found because he hid so well. We'd call his name. We'd say the game was over. We'd say it was time to go home before we got in trouble. And out came the best hider. He would emerge—usually climbing down the tallest tree or crawling out from underneath a dumpster—and we would register his physical-ness. First the outline of his body. Then his individual parts, the fingers, the feet. Then finally his face. His smile. He would be found. He would be part of this world again.

"Breathe deeply," Howard says. "Allow yourself to be only here, in this space."

I would have remained hidden. I would have stayed in my hiding spot for as long as I could, never answering to my name when called, never acknowledging my existence. I would have gladly stayed in the dark. Weeks, months, years. And maybe I would've been forgotten. Maybe I would've become someone's good memory—"Remember that kid Ira? Best hider on the planet." Or, maybe, just maybe, the songs and stories about me would be absent of the word fat, would start first with *he loved the world too much, so he decided to vanish.*

"Open your eyes," Howard says.

The lights come on and the other students gather their things and there I lie, blinded by that sudden change, shocked back in the world, and for a second, just a second, I forget about Body, forget its bulk, until I roll on my side and heave myself up.

♥

Some days I take a shower in the dark. I keep the lights off, bring down the shades over the bathroom window, close the door. Taking a shower in the dark is not a conscious choice. I simply do it, and when the water hits me, when I grope for my shampoo and soap, I wonder why I decided on this act of cleaning myself without light. During these moments I realize Body sometimes makes his own decisions, moves on his own accord, imposes his own will. I read once a man can see a fan spinning and he knows it will hurt but he can't stop his hand from touching the blades anyway. Experts say our bodies react to a set of neurological, psychological, and psychiatric conditions, that showering in the dark is a response to one or all of those conditions. Experts also say there is no difference in showering in the light and showering in the dark. But in the dark, I finally understand how well I know Body. My hand, without any visual cue, washes everything with care and precision, without pause. I slow down. I make sure every inch of Body—the dark crevices below the stomach and in between Body's legs—is covered with soap. In the light, the purpose of showering is to clean. In the dark, the purpose of showering is to explore.

ॐ

We need reasons to explain who we are. We need reasons to explain our choices and decisions—good or bad.

But what if we don't have reasons? What if we stopped going to yoga because it made us too aware of ourselves, because it spotlighted our every flaw, because when we were asked to bend and contort, we couldn't? Instead of finding some sort of peace of mind, we found another activity Body had prevented us from enjoying.

So we stop.

We decide to do nothing. We decide to let Body take over. "Here you go, Body," we say. "Take the helm. Do your baddest." Body has been waiting for this moment. He has been clamoring for this opportunity, and now that he has it, he does nothing. Nothing is the best plan he can think of. Nothing is the fasted route to destruction.

Sometimes he speaks.

Sometimes Body says, "Downward-facing dog. Really?"

Sometimes Body says, "Remember that time you took yoga. What a joke."

So, we spend hours on the couch. We spend hours hating ourselves. We eat and eat and eat. We do this non-stop. We are killing ourselves but we don't know it. We hate ourselves but we don't say it. We want to die but we can't.

One, two, three. Four, five, six years speed by, and we are looking at the scale at the doctor's office. It reads three hundred ninety pounds. We are tired—so, so tired. This is the line we lean on. "How're you feeling?" the doctor says. "Tired," we say. "So, so tired." Could be the pounds we lug around. Could be the blood sugar we can't control. Could be the fact that most days are spent in one place.

We know what the doctor will say: lose weight, exercise. As a joke, we quote Raymond Carver's short story, "Fat." "Believe it or not, we have not always eaten this way." The doctor won't understand; most doctors don't. They are a breed that believes in logic and reason. To them, Body is about cause and effect. Body is about rational decisions. What he doesn't take into account is our mind has become irrational. We ask for anti-depressants. He looks at us and takes note. He asks if we are suicidal. We shake our head. He doesn't believe us. Why should he? Look at us. Look at the fat hanging over the chair. Look at our cheeks, our chins. He signs a prescription pad and then puts a hand on our shoulder. "Try this," he says. "Cut out a picture of a body you admire—a celebrity, perhaps, an athlete—and paste your face to it. Hang it up so you look at it each day. Believe in the power of the mind."

We nod. We say this is a great idea. We thank him for his services.

Outside, the sun beats on us, and it is then we remember one yoga pose: Sun Salutation, a series of twelve moves, consisting of lunging and bending and arching. We never got it right. But it didn't matter. Not that first time. Not any of the times. The point was we made Body move. We made Body realize it could be a flexible vessel, even when our sweat dripped onto the mat, even when our legs trembled, even when our stomach got in the way.

We're not saying this was the moment we would try again. We're not saying we went home and did not eat the mountain mound of rice. We ate. We're not saying we decided not to watch TV and opted for a walk instead. We watched. But something curious happened that day. We took the doctor's advice, but modified it. We took the body we envied—actor Brad Pitt—and cut out Brad's head and put it on our body. And now Brad Sukrungruang was doing the Sun Salutation. And now he was Downward Dogging. And now he was doing a headstand and realized what gravity does with fat. We laughed. Outside, in the summer heat, we laughed. Outside the doctor's office, we laughed. It sounded foreign from our mouth, but familiar, like the word *love* spoken in a different language.

❧

Body says, "Enough."

Body says, "My turn."

Body says, "I've got things to say, too."

Body says, "First, never again eat nacho cheese Combos." He reminds me of that day when we were in first grade and our mother bought Combos for the first time—such an ingenious concept, she thought, a tubular pretzel with cheese in the center—and we kept shoving our hands in the bag and popping them into our mouth.

Body says, "I gave you a warning after the fifteenth one."

Body says, "I learned a valuable lesson that day: you rarely listen." But those Combos, Body goes on, they were heavy in the stomach, so heavy the stomach wanted nothing to do with Combos, so up they came, up through the long and narrow esophagus and through the mouth and onto the green carpeted floor.

Body says, "Would it hurt to eat something green?"

Body knows that when I look in the mirror I see Body and cringe. When Body looks in the mirror, Body sees a boy who still doesn't understand limits, who insists on treating Body as if Body were expendable. Body knows that I am looking to point the finger. This whole essay seems to be an invective against him. He understands it's easy to place blame, to put words in Body's mouth. Body wants to wrap his arm around me, push me into his flesh, two softness-es merging, melding. Body wants to whisper apologies.

Instead, Body says, "I am not to blame. I am only a body."

Body says, "It's time we stop talking."

Body says, "We need to make this work."

Body says, "It's time."

❧

What prompted me to drive to the gym, I don't know. I woke one day in the fall, and instead of finding my spot on the couch, I got into the car, drove three miles east, and found myself in front of a gym. I didn't pause. I didn't hesitate like I had been doing for months, years, talking myself out of it, spinning and spinning my wheels. Perhaps it was the doctor and the diabetes and my wife and family. Perhaps it was vanity—pure vanity—because I would give anything to be skinny just once, to be lithe and bendable like Howard the yoga instructor. Perhaps—and this might be the ironic part—perhaps it was my body that prompted change. Whatever it was, I was in a gym. I was taking aerobic classes. I was losing. Parts of me. Chunks of me. In a year, I lost over a hundred pounds. In a year, I found myself in the yoga studio again. There was a noticeable change in my body. Not just the weight and heft of it. Not just the space I occupied. This was a change that affected the air I took in.

Before she leads us into our first position, Maria, my new yoga instructor in Florida, tells the class to breathe deeply. She says we should prepare our bodies. My mat is in the front of the room. I sit, legs crossed, in baggy basketball shorts and a baseball cap. I take in air through my nostrils. My eyes are closed. I feel the air fill the inner cavity of my nose, feel it spread to every region of my body, down to the tip of my toes. I feel it enter my belly, a cool swirl like a tender wind. I remember once, back in the days when I lived in upstate New York, back when Howard—bearded Howard—was my yoga instructor, I sat in the garden of my house, concentrating on my breath.

Yoga breathing fascinated me. Like walking, I didn't realize there was a right way and a wrong way. But there I sat, eyes shut, breathing in and out. I took five breaths and opened my eyes. The world appeared brighter. Visually stunning. It was as if a gray film had been lifted from my eyes. I held on to this moment for as long I could. I kept breathing—oh the joy of breathing!—and opening my eyes to a feast of color. The world moved, and I understood, only for this moment, that I was connected to it like Howard had been saying. I understood that you couldn't separate mind and body and spirit, that they acted in conjunction with one another. Then I realized I was becoming new agey, and the thought made me self-conscious, and I was back to hating myself.

But I'm allowing for this. I'm allowing for vulnerability. I'm allowing for sadness. You can't stop it. You can only understand it.

Maria stands. I stand. She lifts her right foot. I lift mine. She places it against the other leg. So do I. And then we raise our arms straight into the air, lengthening our spine, opening our chests, our hearts, letting our fingers grow like branches. "Hold that pose," she says. "Feel how rooted you are to the earth." I do. I am a tree, for this moment, standing against a hard wind, knowing I will shake and tremble, but not fall.

Our Next Lives

The train cuts through the flat of central Thailand and the early morning fog. Above us, the sky is thick with lumbering clouds, and the first drop of rain specks the glass. It is the beginning of the rain season, and morning showers are daily occurrences. Rain does not stop the monks, who traverse the countryside with their alms bowls ready for villagers to drop tightly bagged meals. It does not stop the roosters from announcing the coming of the day or the stray dogs that stretch and sniff for their first morsel along the tracks. My mother, leaning on my shoulder, says rain like this is a blessing from Buddha, an assurance of a safe journey.

We head north towards Chiang Mai, the city that will become my mother's future home. For over thirty years, she worked as a nurse and lived in Chicago, and since her retirement, she has been planning her return; America was only a workplace, never a permanent stop.

Even though this is one of many trips to Thailand since I was three, I have always been fixated by the landscape. The expanse of green is nothing like the pastures in rural Illinois, nothing like the prairies of Kansas or Nebraska. This is a lush and wet green, a wild green, a green that devours. So much of it is hypnotic, makes you want to disappear into the pigment.

When we zoom past water buffalo, my mother points and says the word for water buffalo in Thai, *kwai*. When we pass a bunch of lotuses blooming in an irrigation ditch, she points and says the word for lotuses, *dok bwua*. For the next few hours, before the land begins to climb up the mountains of the north and the earth becomes rich and red, she points and names. This activity does not bore her. She can do this until we arrive at our destination or when she succumbs to an afternoon nap.

I wonder, in her recitation, whether she is doing it more for herself than me, whether each object or animal or plant she sees in a blur is a remembrance of the life she once knew, a past life, a much younger one when all she thought about during her days were not of paying her son's college tuition or calculating the right meds for patients, but of climbing rubber trees or diving off bridges into the murky creeks below.

"This is how we say in Thai," she says again and again. "*Dok gulaab.* Rose. *Ling.* Monkey. *Nok.* Bird."

I nod, my eyes fixed on the passing green.

I know the names of all the things my mother points at. I've known for years, but decide not to disrupt her. These are the moments, I believe, my mother still hopes for: the opportunity to teach and pass something important down to her twenty-eight year-old son, to impart a lesson that will resonate in his next life.

❧

Throughout my childhood, my mother often spoke of our future lives. This talk made its way into our daily language. Unlike my friends whose parents threatened them with punishments of groundings or two weeks of no Nintendo, my mother's threats were not immediate. If I were caught in a lie, my mother would say I would be reborn as a laugh-less hyena. If I didn't stop eating, I would be sent back as a pig ready for slaughter. If I received another B- in Math, I would be the monkey who ate its own feces. For a child of five or six, such threats were effective. Nothing put more fear into me than the thought of returning as a worm I liked to split in half with my sneakers.

The older I became, however, my mother's threats were of little consequence to me. My imagination created stories of my would-be future lives. If I were a pig, then I would be like Wilbur the pig in E.B. White's *Charlotte's Web*, who, in the end, escaped the fate of the axe. If I came back as a worm, I would be the one that aerated the soil for the largest tomatoes this world would ever see. No matter how disgusting my mother described my next life, in my mind I found ways to make whatever I would become pleasant, to give it reason, to give it purpose.

❧

It is spring, and spring always warrants conversations of rebirth. My wife Katie and I are in our garden in upstate New York. My mother will be arriving in a few days for a visit with her only son and white wife, who, according to her, is very Thai and thus deemed acceptable. Katie and I do regular maintenance to the garden, making sure we've pulled out all the weeds, planting annuals in the empty spaces, and mulching. Though we do not say it, we work quickly and thoroughly knowing my mother loves to spend time on one of the Adirondack chairs in the early morning with her cup of instant coffee. This will be her last visit before returning home.

Katie believes there is a purpose to almost every living thing on this planet. Even though she was born in a Christian family—she claims no affinity towards any religion—she is more Buddhist than some of the monks I've known through all my years of attending Wat Dhammaram, the Thai Buddhist temple of Chicago.

As we work I ask the purpose of a few of my least favorite insects. "How about spiders?" I say and shiver. I am a bit arachnophobic.

"They keep flies and mosquitoes in check," says Katie.

"All right, mosquitoes. What possible purpose do they serve in life?"

This one Katie takes a while to answer. She places snapdragons next to the red mini-rose. "To make you miserable."

"That's a cop out."

"Fine. Birds eat them. Swallows. Purple Martins."

I dig out a spent dandelion. "My mother thinks the things that inconvenience us, that cause us angst, are part of life, too."

"Isn't that a Buddhist concept? Suffering?"

"Hell yeah it is."

Katie mulches her new plantings, while I get the hose ready to water.

"What would you choose to be if it came down to a mosquito and spider?" she says.

Not many weeks ago, I read an article about the largest spider web found in America. It was in Texas and was as big as a football field. The reporter described the web as fairy tale white. Though I loathed and feared spiders—something my mother thinks I acquired in a prior life; perhaps I had been bitten by one and died—to be that particular spider, to spin that web, would be a life well spent. I tell Katie so.

"That," my wife says, "is true purpose."

I ask her if she would like to be born as *her* biggest fear: June bugs.

"Not in a million years. I hate those fuckers."

❧

While surfing the internet, I found a website called Reincarnation Station. It's a simple site that has a simple quiz you can take to find out what you would be in the future. I do not remember the exact questions, but some were about personality, like, *Are you a social person?* Others were simple what-ifs? *What if you only had two dollars and a friend asked to borrow exactly two dollars, what would you do?* After answering about ten questions, Reincarnation Station took twenty seconds to calculate that I would return as a rhino, which meant, according to the website, that 27% of people will be reincarnated as a higher form of life than me.

❧

The trip to Chiang Mai is about twelve hours long. We are halfway there. The rain ceased an hour ago, but my mother hasn't stopped pointing and naming. In the states, when we were in the station wagon, she would read every sign or billboard we passed. Younger, this was our favorite pastime. We went from block to block, yelling out the name of streets and the numbers on mailboxes, smiling and laughing as I leaned against her chest. Then I didn't correct her English. Didn't criticize how she never rolled her R's. When I became an insubordinate teenager, I found the game childish and complained. I was a complaining master. I told my mother she was annoying. I told her her English was atrocious. I told her she was acting like a child. This, however, only made her do it louder.

Once I asked her why—besides getting on my last nerve—she insisted on reading every thing we passed?

"Practice English. Learn by saying out loud. Good for memory."

In the train, my mother has stopped trying to teach me the Thai words for the world outside, not because I wasn't listening, but because, for her, this repetition became an act of relearning, and perhaps, an act of reliving. Lulled by the sound of the tracks and the occasional burst from the train horn, my mother reacquaints herself with Thailand, not as someone who took six-week vacations every other year to visit family, but one who is preparing for a permanent stay. She speaks more to herself, under her breath. Thai words slip through her lips in a barely audible whisper, like a blossoming prayer.

Despite myself, I want to hear her voice. I want to be that child again, cuddled against her chest, sing-songing every road sign, every number on a mailbox. But those moments are lost, tangled in the wild green of memory.

‿

"I know I am deathless . . . ," Walt Whitman wrote in "Song of Myself," "We have thus far exhausted trillions of winters and summers, there are trillions ahead, and trillions ahead of them."

We measure time in seasons. We cross off days on a calendar, watch ourselves age in the mirror—one new wrinkle, one new gray, one less strand of hair. We wait for indications in the sky, the fluctuating temperature of the wind, to tell us that, yes, we are indeed moving forward; yes, the world around us is evolving as steadily as we are.

But we come back.

We live again.

It is a continuous cycle.

My father might have been Whitman in a former life, if he wasn't already positive he was born the same type of man each and every time. He claims to have always been a soldier. In his sleep, sometimes he hears the clashing of swords, feels the undulating motion of going to battle atop a great elephant. He tells me he always died tragically but honorably.

In this life, however, he was a wanderer, and it was his wandering that eventually led him onto a different path from my mother and me. Like Whitman, my father loved words, though he never wrote anything other than chemical equations and numbers on fortune telling grids. When he wasn't a tile chemist, he made extra money as a fortune teller.

Once, when I was eight, I followed him to a Thai restaurant on the north side of Chicago. The owner of the restaurant was having a difficult time staying out of the red, and he hoped my father could help with his future.

When we arrived at the restaurant, it was desolate, but immaculately decorated. I felt as if I had walked into a temple in Thailand, with angels dancing across colorful Thai silk, the candles flickering off the jeweled inlets in the walls. The owner had whipped up a feast for us: stir-fried chicken, beef and potato curry stew, scrambled eggs with crabmeat, cellophane noodles with jumbo shrimp cooked in a clay pot. He was a kind man, the owner, with mournful eyes. He possessed the look and build of a Thai Mister Rogers.

As I ate bowl after bowl of rice, my father said it wasn't the owner's future that was the problem. It was his past, his former lives. The same wrong was repeating itself over and over again. My father went on to describe what had happened in the man's former life in vague details: he had spent too much money on a dream that didn't come to fruition, that eventually this dream sapped him of all he had—his house, his wife and kids, and eventually his life.

Similarly, in 1980, psychologist Dr. Brian Weiss met a new patient, twenty-seven-year-old Catherine, who suffered from severe panic attacks. His experiences with Catherine are recounted in his book, *Many Lives, Many Masters*. Dr. Weiss decided to use nontraditional forms of therapy, like hypnosis, to uncover regressed or blocked memory. What he found astounded him. Catherine not only recalled events in her current life, but ones from her other lives. She stated that she had lived eighty-six times. She even remembered how she died in some of them—stabbed, drowned, illness. The causes of Catherine's panic attacks were not solely because of her current past, but unresolved issues in her former lives.

The restaurant owner was suffering the same fate. "What should I do?" he asked, sighing heavily. This poor man had spent an hour listening to my father, hanging on his every word because when my father spoke, most of the time, excluding my mother, people listened.

"Sell this restaurant," my father said with confidence. "Open a small gas station."

I do not remember what happened to the man, whether he was able to break the cycle and live a happy life, whether my father helped him in the least. But what I heard that afternoon stayed with me. I began to wonder if I was making the same mistake, whether I suffered the same anxieties as I did before, like poor Catherine, like my mother's theory for my fear of spiders. I wondered if one could be stuck living the same tragic life over and over again.

It was a distressing thought. I did not dwell on it too long.

જ

There is no real scientific or religious answer on how one becomes reincarnated. No easy step-by-step guide. There has been talk of a light. There has been talk of a waiting room where the soul prepares to plunge into another body. There has been talk of doing good deeds in life to accumulate a wealth of karma, which will spill over into the next existence. Every text

I have read is riddled with theory and philosophy, thick and dense and head-spinningly confusing. His Holiness the Dalai Lama says that when his soul departs his physical body it will house itself into another; it will be up to his disciples to find him again. This, I imagine, would be a tough job.

For a long time, I was under the assumption that, once dead, we could hand pick what we wanted to become. Maybe it was not an assumption. It was my hope.

To be reincarnated seemed almost like preparing for Halloween. When I was younger, Halloween was serious business. Ideas about the next costume happened the day after October 31. It was a year-long process where I began to jot down all the characters I wished to become. There were infinite options on what one would want to be.

Here are the odd numbered years:

At three: Chewy, from *Star Wars*.

Five: Darth Vader.

Seven: Luke Skywalker.

Nine: The basketball great, Larry Bird. (On a side note, I had two costumes that year. My mother entered me in a costume contest at temple as a rice field worker. I took first prize, beating out Ananya the Nurse.)

Eleven: Yoda, Jedi Master.

Your decision about what to become in your next life would be like deciding on a costume, only you had a lifetime to ponder, to really think things through. And when the moment comes, your soul will rise into the sky, and arrive at a place in the clouds. Do not worry; it will seem like you are on a 1983 B-movie set, with a fog machine hidden somewhere. And behind that fog you will find a man in a waiter's outfit, ready to take your order, pen poised above a pad.

This has been the moment you have planned for your entire life.

"Plant or animal," he says.

"Animal," you say.

"Species of choice?"

"Human."

"Gender?"

"Flip a coin."

"Where would you like to be born?"

"In a galaxy far, far away."

ↄ

The Sufi poet Rumi wrote: "I died as a mineral and became a plant, I died as a plant and rose to animal, I died as animal and I was a man." But when you died as a man, Rumi, what was there left to become?

ↄ

Chiang Mai will be the beginning of my mother's third life. In the first one, she was a girl who paddled to school in a canoe, who listened to bombs falling on Bangkok during WWII, who accepted her nursing degree from the Queen of Thailand. Her second life is one of disappointment, of homesickness, and according to her, of her greatest joy. Here she woke up each day in a country where she felt lost. Here she loved and learned heartbreak. Here she gave birth to a son, who kept always close to her side.

Now, beyond the train window, she can see her new life approaching. In this life she vows to do nothing but read and relax. In this life, she says she will travel to all the places she's never been—India, China, Laos, Singapore, Australia. In this life, she will no longer speak English or shop at grocery stores with mediocre produce and packaged meats; it will be Thai, only Thai, and open-air markets. In this life, she will see her son every other year for two to three months at a time, and when he is back in the states she will call once a week. In this life, she will prepare for the next one, whenever that may be.

The train slows. The mountains of Thailand are not like the jagged and rocky peaks of the Himalayas. There are no snowy peaks, no slate gray rock. These are jungled mountains; they begin like the gentle curve of a tortoise shell, swaying up and down, higher and higher. Despite the change in landscape, the green doesn't leave us. It follows.

Since we left Bangkok early this morning, my mother keeps her eyes pointed out the window. When the train descends into a valley, my mother nudges my arm and points at a giant golden Buddha, shining mid-mountain in the distance. The Buddha is striking amidst the green. He looms large, facing the direction we just traveled. His eyes are half open, and I wonder if he is waking up or falling asleep. The setting sun reflects off his gold skin, as a few sparrows fly from his meditating palms.

"Pay respect," my mother says. She puts her hands together, and I do the same. Every Buddha we pass she always instructs me to pay my respects, even the fat ones we find in Chicago's Chinatown, even the ones we see at gaudy souvenir stores. I've become accustomed to this ritual. My mother believes with every show of respect, we attain good karma.

I want my mother's new life in Chiang Mai to make up for all her disappointments. I want her new life to be filled with happiness.

"Pray," she says.

I do.

"Ask for good fortune. Ask for comfort. Ask—"

I know the script well, but this time, before my mother finishes her last request, I do it for her. "Ask for another life together."

Please Don't Talk About It

I

The dog, my dog, lies in the shape of a crescent moon, her front and back paws curling towards each other. She dreams, I am sure, of her greatest moment—the day she brought back a decomposing deer leg. She was not over two then, just a pup, and the leg was twice—maybe three times—the length of her spaniel body. What must she have thought when she came upon such a discovery? What joy did it bring her? She emerged from the expanse of Illinois grass that towered over her a champion, hefting the weight of that deer leg in her small mouth, dragging it to us, breathing in short audible bursts through her nose.

I don't remember who took it from her, who was brave enough to touch the dried and crusted flank. But I do remember how my dog offered the leg as a gift. How she expended so much energy to bring it to us, this dead and rotting leg. How she did not stay in that field, hidden by prairie grass, and feast.

This is what I think about as I watch her sleep, eight years later. There is more white under her chin and her eyes have become cloudier. And in those years she has given us more presents: a dead and frozen Downy woodpecker, mice, a vole, a rabbit, unfortunate squirrels.

Her paws twitch.

Her mouth twitches.

She makes tiny squeaks.

In her dreams, she is off—the ageless dog—scampering across endless flat fields after prey that can never escape her boundless energy.

II

We joke, my wife Katie and I, about my upcoming death.

"Don't you dare die," she says. "We don't have life insurance on you yet."

"I've been feeling pain in my left arm." I grab my chest dramatically. "And my heart hurts."

"If you die, I swear I'll kick your ass."

"I'll try to hold off a little longer, but no guarantees."

"I'm just saying I need that insurance money."

We joke. This type of joking is almost a daily routine, and because it is routine, it is, in fact, a real issue, with real fears. Because underneath our banter is the recognition that I will die. Perhaps sooner than most. Because I am over three hundred pounds and in love with starches and deep-fried food. Because I am a diabetic. Because, though I exercise, I eat more than my body can contain. Because my body is finally feeling youth slip away and suddenly my knees/back/ankles/hips hurt. Because now, I pay for my late nights.

Sometimes joking about what we fear most is the only way to confront it.

When we finally get life insurance, Katie says, "OK, you can die now."

"I'll pencil it in."

"Maybe next year," she says. "I get more money the longer you last."

III

Lord Buddha: How many times do you think about death?
Monk Number 1: I think about death every day.
Lord Buddha: Too little. How about you?
Monk Number 2: I think about death with every bite of food.
Lord Buddha: Not enough. And you?
Monk Number 3: I think about death with every breath in and every breath out.
Lord Buddha: Perfect.

IV

And then there are conversations. Somehow when it gets to be a certain hour of night, my friend and I speak only of dying. We speak about loss. We speak in hushed tones, afraid if we get louder someone will hear us, two tough boys being open, being vulnerable. Or worse yet, we don't want our talk to be omens.

My friend is layered in muscle. He works at the lumber yard at night, and spends his afternoons in the gym pumping iron. He takes supplements, drinks protein shakes, and is a carb-eating machine. He also deals. Heroin, coke, 'roids. He doesn't talk about that stuff with me, even if we're best friends. I don't ask, even when I want to know.

He leans against my minivan in the garage, and the summer night brings the song of crickets. He says, "Crickets live less than a year."

"Mr. Science," I say.

"Longer if they stay warm."

"Look at you," I say. "The Polish fact machine."

He chuckles and stretches his right bicep, as big as my head. "What would you do if you had a year to live?"

I shrug. "Lots, I guess." The truth: probably the same thing I do now. Sit outside listening to crickets with him. When you're nineteen, what else is better?

"I'd stop working out," he says. "I'd stop doing any sort of exercise."

I make a sound that says *whatever*. My friend is obsessive about the gym. If he's not there, he's at work. If he's not at work, he's in my garage talking about dying. I can't imagine him without dumbbells in his hands. I mean, this is the guy who bought an electric contraption to shock his muscles into shape.

"For real," my friend says. He flexes his left arm. "You know how much time I put in to make these?" He flexes his right. He lifts his shirt to show me his abdominals.

"A lot of time," I say. I have the opposite body. Fat and flabby. I slouch on an aluminum chair.

"I work out more than I sleep." My friend yawns. "If I had a year to live, I'd stop doing anything healthy."

"You can stop now," I say. "Take a few days off."

He smirks. He thinks what I've said is absurd.

"I can't stop," he says.

"Why?"

"I'm afraid."

"The irony." My friend admits his time at the gym is to stave off death. He keeps his body in prime condition so it can fight off sickness and age. What he doesn't know is that longevity and living are two different things. What he doesn't know is the stuff he pops and drinks are poison. What he doesn't know is that dying happens to the healthy too. Dying happens to everyone.

My friend says, "A cricket is loudest right before it dies."

"Did you make that up?"

He smiles and says, "Trust a Polak."

V

They were uneven, those stitches, like railroad tracks drawn in a clumsy hand, arcing across the curve of her stomach. *It doesn't hurt*, she said. *I don't know they're there at all.* I wanted to ride across her wound with my fingers, to understand why she had been gone for so long while I waited and watched, closing and opening my eyes, thinking she might appear in her usual spots: by the window sewing, upstairs reading a Thai magazine, under Buddha sipping coffee. I called for her, louder and louder each time. The neighborhood echoed with my voice. She never came. I feared losing her then, and knew I would keep losing her—each minute, each second—knew that even then as I hid my face in her hair, ashamed of the wet coming from my eyes, wondering about what other things we were going to lose, what other things had already been lost. *What will you do?* she said and has been saying for thirty years, her hand hovering over the stitches. *What will you do when I am gone?*

VI

I concentrate on breathing. I count my breaths. I prevent anything from entering my mind. Sometimes it works. Sometimes it fails. When it fails, I toss and turn. I sigh loudly. My wife lying beside me tells me to "settle" in the same stern voice she uses with our dogs when they howl at a cat. Sorry, I tell her, and lay board still, my body tight, like one united muscle. I concentrate on her breathing. I count her breaths. But my mind, my damn mind, has gone to the places I do not want it to tread. Fear clenches my body. I shut my eyes. I shake my head. I try to disrupt my thoughts with movement. But my mind imagines a life without. Without my wife. Without my mother. Without all of those I love. I panic. My hands ball up. My toes curl tight. I take shallow breaths. And my heart. It thuds in my chest so loud and fast I think this could be it, the heart attack I have been waiting for.

This. Is. It.

I'm dying.

I'm not.

I play games to chase the fear away. *Imagine yourself eating your favorite food. Imagine the taste of that food. Imagine the joy of eating that food.* Or, *picture yourself snorkeling some unknown sea. Picture yourself among so many colorful fish. Picture yourself as one of the colorful fish.* Sometimes it works. Sometimes it fails. When it fails, I am frozen and sweating and clutching the covers tight in both hands. Waiting.

VII

I should be ready for this. I'm counting down.

VIII

My wife had an addiction to this TV series that appeared on cable, *Dead Like Me*. The show was about Reapers, who were once part of the living but now worked at the business of Death. Each day, Reapers met in a greasy-spoon diner, and the head Reaper—played by the charismatic Mandy Patinkin—gave out Post-It notes with a first initial and last name and also the time and place the Reaper had to be to claim the soul. *Dead Like Me* took the scythe and black hood away from Death, and gave the job to a mix of crazy characters. The series showcased inventive and outrageous ways people died. Example: the main character, George, was killed by a space station toilet seat plummeting to the earth. Those were my favorite parts, those eccentric deaths.

Most of the time, however, the series centered on George. She hated her job of taking souls. Understandably. But George also clung hard to her former life. She followed her younger sister around in her new unrecognizable body. She kept breaking into her old house and leaving clues to her existence. She couldn't let go. Even in death, she was suffering from her former life, which as a Buddhist scared the hell out of me.

Buddhists believe in leaving no footprint, but a great majority of us do just that. We want to be remembered. We want to remember. I'm always struck by the question, "How do you want people to remember you?" Often this is asked of celebrities, politicians, the rich and famous. And often, the answer is stock: "As a good father." Or, "A person who gave." Or, "A person who tried hard." Not once have I heard, "I don't."

But on a minor scale, we ask ourselves this very question every day—not straightforwardly, not directly—but it is implicit in our daily routines, the decisions we make, the people we keep company with. It is in many ways, why some of us collect things, why some of us can't throw things away. Who will remember us if we don't leave these clues? Who will speak of us when we are gone? I wonder whether being alive is about being remembered.

George the Reaper says: "We lead our lives, and when they end, sometimes we leave a little of ourselves behind. Sometimes we leave money, a painting, sometimes we leave a kind word. And sometimes, we leave an empty space."

IX

My mother tells me we live this life for our next lives, and I wonder if that's living. Since I can remember, she has said over and over again it *is* happening. She talks about her death in the present tense. Present tense, at this moment, right now. I remember her saying this when I was seven. She continues to say this.

It is happening.

She's right, of course. The moment we are born, we are dying. Our cells are moving and changing by the nanosecond. Young, we don't care. We don't feel it. We don't register time because there are so many things to do, so many things left to accomplish. Too much fun to be had. But at a certain age, time registers. Suddenly the phrases, "Time flew by, didn't it?" or, "I can't believe the year is over" creep in to our language. Suddenly we recognize—though many of us don't want to—that we have expiration dates.

My mother knows this. She has known this for a good many years, even though many of her family lived well into their nineties. She wants me to know it to. She wants me to be aware of it myself.

It is happening.

X

"The vampires have it bad," a girl I dated once said. "All they do is suffer. They can never experience the ecstasy of mortality. They're denied death."

"Unless you have a wooden stake," I said. "Some holy water, too, and a good dose of sunshine."

I met her in debate class in my freshman year of college, and we dated for a week because we didn't know what to do with ourselves. Meeting in debate meant we were always on opposite sides of an issue. Abortion: she found it unholy; I was for a woman's right to choose. Capital punishment: she was for death to criminals; I was for life sentences with possibility of parole. In that week of our intimacy, the topic we often circled around was death. She was obsessed by it, knew bizarre death facts.

"A cockroach can live without a head. True story. Then it starves."

"There was a news reporter who killed herself on the air. True story. Boom, gun shot in the head."

"Tennessee Williams died—true story—because he choked on a bottle cap."

After a few days, I couldn't take any more true stories. She wasn't a goth girl. There were plenty of them on campus, wandering like zombies in tight groups, usually English majors. She didn't listen to death metal. She didn't stare off into space or mumble incantations. She appeared to be typical. A blue jeans and sweatshirt kinda girl. Someone you wouldn't mind bringing home to meet Mom and Dad.

Except the death thing.

Her fascination scared me, made me look for death at every turn. When I crossed the street, I made sure no car came because, according to her, four thousand pedestrians died a year in auto-related accidents. When I ate, I chewed carefully with the knowledge that two thousand people died last year alone because of choking. I smoked less because she liked to describe the lungs of a dead smoker.

It didn't occur to me that her infatuation with death might have been a telltale sign of depression. I was barely eighteen, self-centered, and my first year of college had been rough, and here was this girl in debate who intrigued me with her arguments in class, even though I disagreed with everything she said.

Finally, during lunch at the cafeteria, I said, "Can't we talk about butterflies and bunnies?'

"They die, too, you know," she said, chewing a chicken tender.

"Please don't talk about this anymore."

"OK," she said.

"Let's try something else."

But there was nothing else to talk about, and without her talk of death, there was nothing between us at all. We sat in silence, eating our lunches.

When she was done, she rose with her tray and said, "You should try being a vampire."

XI

Lord Buddha says, "Do not mourn me." He lies supine under a Bodhi tree that is shaped like an umbrella. Monks have gathered around their teacher. The young ones pat away moisture from their eyes. The older ones are resolute. They wait for one last lesson.

Lord Buddha says, "This is a joyous moment." His body begins to glow. There was one other time his body lit up like this. The moment of Enlightenment.

Lord Buddha says, "I will be free of this body that housed suffering." He closes his eyes. Ready.

XII

Lately, I've had this urge to document everything. Wherever I go, I take a picture. Usually, it is of something that moves me. The light between trees. Pelicans and cormorants on a dock. Sunlight off a pond. Sometimes, I set the timer on my camera and pose dramatically. I think about my poses. I think about my facial expression. My poses are usually silly. I stick my tongue out. I play a role, like a quick-shot cowboy or gang-sta. These pictures aren't for me. They're never for me. They're for my wife. My family. My friends. I want them to remember me and the things I love in case I'm not there anymore to tell them why I love these things. When I get home, I rush to the computer. I make sure to organize my photos into folders labeled by the date. This is important. Again, it's not for me.

You can know my days by what pictures I take. You can know my life by what faces I make. If something happens, there is evidence that I exist. If something happens . . .

XIII

In W. S. Merwin's poem "For the Anniversary of My Death," Merwin writes: "Every year without knowing it I have passed the day...." I always pause at that line. Its profoundness takes my breath away. We wake up each day and fill it with activity. At the end of the day, some of us will sleep and wake again, and some of us will continue sleeping. The poet Cesar Vallejo wrote in his poem "Black Stone Lying on a White Stone" that his death would come on a Thursday. "I will die in Paris—and I don't step aside—perhaps on a Thursday, as today is Thursday, in autumn." Vallejo died, for the record, on a Friday in spring.

These poets and many more who have broached the topic of death have gotten me thinking about the cliché, Death follows you. And I'm not sure Death follows anyone. I think, in fact, you follow death.

Recently, I listened to my sister-in-law, who is in seminary school, speak at her father's memorial service. In the soft cadence of her voice, in her pointed prose, I was struck by the details of his life, his joys, his happiness. He was a man who lived, who loved, and was loved. And perhaps, I'm rationalizing, but I am empowered by this sentiment. My sister-in-law's speech on that gusty Illinois afternoon spoke of living regardless of religious affiliation or lack thereof.

Buddha, the poet, said: "If we keep death in front of us, if we are aware of it, we will live better lives."

Before Buddha closed his eyes, before he gave in to his death, what was it, I wonder, he saw? Was it a bird trilling in the tree? Was it his disciples' orange robes fluttering in the wind? Was it the sunlight peeking through branches? I would like to think before his last breath he saw the shape of contentment, and that contentment would guide him into whatever his next life would be.

For the time being, for me, this must suffice.

The Usual Spots

I

Every morning, the dogs look for Katie in the usual places. When I open the bedroom door, they burst through the house in tongue-wagging hopefulness. Perhaps the one they truly love has returned from whatever mysterious place she disappears to most of the week. I wonder what that place is to them, wonder if they have created a second life for her, where she wakes and loves and pats other dogs. Are these the dreams they have when they snarl and twitch and sometimes howl in their sleep?

The morning always brings hope, and it is a mad dash into her empty office, then a rumble down the basement stairs, and finally a quick peek out the front windows where she would spend time filling birdfeeders or watering the flower beds. Once they have confirmed that she is not back—not yet—they do not despair. Never despair. They rush out the dog door to tend to morning routines, while I fill their bowls with food.

They are not the only ones who wait. I find myself forgetting at times that she is not here, that for this year she is teaching four days of the week at another university three hours away. While watching a TV show, I laugh, point, and say to the empty spot on the couch, "Wasn't that funny?" Or suddenly, while making a snack, I shout over the hum of the refrigerator, "Help me find the jam."

At night, the dogs and I take our usual positions in bed. I occupy the right side, and the dogs nestle into their spots—on the pillow beside her head, the space that the crook of her knees would make. While there is so much room on the king-sized bed, none of us creep over to where she would be. That place remains vacant, like a missing puzzle piece. The dogs and I hope she will return and occupy that spot, and then my hand, which is often lonely at night, will find the swale of her hip.

II

It has been a year of changes and adjustments. Besides Katie accepting a teaching job three hours away, this summer, after the school year, we are moving from the hills of upstate New York to the lush flatness of Florida, and this past November, my wife's mother, Dinny, passed away from pancreatic cancer.

For so long Dinny has been what signified home for Katie. It was not the flat of the Midwest or the horses grazing in some pasture that she often reminisced about; it was a woman who talked her through the most difficult of times, a woman who always remained level-headed and rational, a consistent presence in Katie's life.

Months after Dinny's death, my wife still looks for her. Her number remains in Katie's cell phone, and once, while driving three hours home, she accidently called it, thinking she could pass the time by talking to her mother. There are other times she forgets. During college basketball season, especially when the University of Illinois's Fighting Illini are on court, any major tennis tournament, and the Westminster Dog Show at Madison Square Garden. And when Katie remembers, her chest is heavy, laden with loss.

We have inherited much of her stuff. Her recliner, which has become "my" chair. But often, I can still see her in it, peeling a juicy pear. Her desk, where recently Katie pulled out a small drawer and found a note that said, "I love you! –Mom Pom." Her polar fleeces, her lamps, her jewelry. Her night light, her kitchen utensils, her photo albums. Her old letters, her blankets, her sweet dog.

In death, we become infused in objects and familiar places. Our loved ones see not a tree, but us climbing the tree. They see not a canoe, but us in it, coasting down some Colorado River, fishing for trout. They see not the backyard, but us on our knees in the backyard planting the petunias. It is what haunts Katie; it is what pulls at her heart. Though she speaks of her mother in the past tense, she still looks for her in the usual spots.

III

I have been watching ghost hunting shows on TV. It's my secret vice, an obsession I don't like to admit to, and when I do I laugh and say, "It's stupid, but I can't help myself." Regardless, on Wednesdays, I hunch in front of the television to watch ghost hunters walk around century-old houses, decrepit prisons, old theaters with EMF meters and digital recorders.

According to many paranormal researchers, there are two main types of hauntings. An "intelligent haunting" simply means a paranormal experience that responds and interacts with the living. You wave at it, it waves back. And though I love when these hauntings happen—it heightens up the drama; makes me sit at the edge of my seat—the more common type of haunting is "residual," where an entity relives an event over and over. Most of the time, this event occurs at the same time, and the "ghost" does not respond or even acknowledge that the living are there; it simply proceeds with its daily life, as if the world had not changed. It knows not of the wall you put up to split up the kitchen and dining room. It does not know that the vanity mirror it so longingly sat at was auctioned off on eBay years ago. It only knows routine.

You don't need to be a ghost to understand the comforts of a routine. For years, between the ages of six and ten, I waited for my father to come home from work at exactly 11:28 every evening. If he stopped for chicken wings, he'd arrive home at 11:41. I knew the sound his Oldsmobile station wagon made, knew the thud and rattle as it drove up the cracked driveway. I listened for the garage door to lift, for the station wagon to come to a stop, then the door to close again. It wouldn't take long before he shuffled down the steps to the back door and emerged through the laundry room, where I'd be waiting for him, arms crossed behind my back, beaming at his return. He'd make an exasperated sound, a sharp intake of breath, as if I was a ghost that seemed to materialize from air. I shouldn't be up, he'd say. A young boy like me should be in bed, he'd say. But my father would be smiling, glad I was there, knowing I'd be waiting.

We expected to see each other. His return each evening was the completion of my day. If he was late—and he seldom was—I would find myself in a state of panic, thinking the worst, needing my father to calm me when he'd eventually arrive home.

For me and my immigrant parents, routine took precedent. I lived in accordance with The Rules posted on the refrigerator door, rules that instructed me on what time I should brush my teeth and how often I should bathe; but also, The Rules advised me on how to be a proper Thai boy. Routine is what drove my mother and father to rise like clockwork to go to work, always taking the same streets, always utilizing the same lanes. My family shopped only on Mondays and Thursdays at The Jewel, the local grocery chain. On Saturdays, we made our way to Chinatown for dim sum, picked up a few items from the Asian grocery store, and brought home roasted duck, crispy pork, and soy sauce chicken from Wing Chun's for dinner. On Sundays it was temple.

Routine meant we made it through another day in a country that scared the hell out of us. If something disrupted that routine, it was yet another obstacle to overcome, another shadow of doubt about whether this was truly home.

IV

I expect the autumn to bring apples. I expect the tornado sirens to go off when the Midwest sky turns green. When I was sixteen, I expected to see my mother parked at the sewing machine after I arrived home from school. I expect

Katie to fall asleep while I watch my ghost hunting shows. I expect the dogs to greet me each and every time I enter the house with toys stuffed in their spaniel mouths. When my mother calls from Thailand, I expect her to ask me if I've eaten. When my father calls from Thailand, I expect him to ask for money. Each morning, I expect to see Katie drink her same tea—Earl Grey decaf—and eat her same peanut butter-smeared toast. The dogs expect to be fed at 6:30 A.M. and 5:30 P.M. They also expect a lot of Milkbones in between. I expect one of them to sleep under my desk as I write. I expect the other to be with my wife as she writes. We expect the earth to continually rotate around the sun, and the sun to continually warm and give life to our planet. We expect to age, day by day. We expect to see the light in the morning and the dark at night.

V

Six years ago, Dinny told Katie and her brother John their old house in White Heath, Illinois, was for sale. This house that I've heard so much about was the center of Katie's childhood. All her joys and fondest memories revolved around White Heath. Moving from it was like an exodus.

Because we were in town for a visit, Dinny scheduled an appointment to see the house. She had no intentions of buying it. Already, her knees were giving out, and it would have been tough to negotiate the stairs and keep up the maintenance on the barn and mow the pasture. It was only a trip to see what had changed, to see where their lives used to be.

When John pulled into the driveway, I became witness to the life of a family I knew very little about. I understood this moment. It's the same when I return to Chicago, and I begin to point out the places I hung out, kissed a girl, caused mischief. Immediately the siblings darted out of the car like they were seven, pointing and talking a mile a minute about the places they hid and played and rode the horses.

"The trees, man, they've grown," said John. John wore a Savoy Firefighter T-shirt. He dreamt of being fireman then and was one now.

"Your father and I planted the pines," Dinny said.

"They were tiny," said Katie.

"Not anymore," said Dinny. "I wish Chip and Dorey could see this."

The trees and the overgrowth in the pasture seemed to be the only change. The house, Katie told me, looked exactly the same. Two-story. Green. A barn and horse ring. I followed like a ghost from one place to the other, listening in on their pasts.

Every inch of the house was a memory.

"Remember how we had to feed the horses in the morning?"

"Remember how we had to get the ice out of the water buckets in the winter?"

"Remember how your father built the stalls?"

In the living room: "Remember how Grandmommy drank bourbon every evening here?"

In the dining room: "Remember how Chip blamed the broken window on the dog?"

In the boys' bedroom: "Remember how Dorey pulled Chip's ears, trying to make him a Vulcan?"

In the girls' bedroom: "Remember, after Dorey's accident, she wanted her big toe kissed?

Katie and John, despite the years, knew this house like the blood in their veins. When they opened the closet door where they used to hide from the tornadoes, they saw their names in pencil still on the wood ceiling.

Dinny stayed a few steps behind, and I imagined this was what she did back then, always a few steps behind in order to see where her children were. The sight of this house seemed to give her the energy she didn't have. Seemed to straighten her walk to the point she didn't need her cane. Seemed to remind her of the mother she once was, the Morgan horse trainer she used to be. Now, for only this hour, she was resuming her role again.

John and Katie could've stayed there forever. They could've slipped back into their routines without skipping a beat. It would be summer and the two of them, the youngest of the siblings, would run into the pasture to bring Crest, Diamond, and Lady in for the day, and later, Katie would slip out again, crawl under the grape vines to her secret spot, the big tree in the Wild Area, she called it, a place to sneak away from the world of grown-ups, a place where no one would find her, but her mother's voice calling her back home.

"All right, kids," Dinny said after an hour, "It's time."

And like they did then, I assumed, following the command and comfort of their mother's voice, John and Katie promptly got into the car and slowly drove away, Katie looking back until the pines, which had grown so tall, were tiny like how she remembered them.

VI

Since moving back to Thailand in 2004, my mother has begun another life. She has left America behind her. It is as if she had never lived in Illinois, never worked as a nurse for thirty years in Chicago, never raised and packed her son's lunch for grade school. She has severed her life there, and when she calls now, she tells me of her life in Thailand, and it is dissimilar from the life she left.

What I know of her is the woman who used to live here. I know of the sad woman. The fearful one. The disappointed one. I know of the woman who sewed every day after the divorce. I know of her playfulness, her times when she was a not a mother, but a child herself. I know what scared her most here. I know what gave her the most joy. I know where to search for her—by the bay windows overlooking the neighborhood, in the backyard hanging clothes, in the kitchen chair facing the stove reading a Thai magazine. I know how to contact her, how to get to her if I needed to. I know what McDonald's meal she liked and her favorite steakhouse on Cicero Avenue.

Since her move, I am learning her new life. I am relearning my mother.

VII

Moving is an act of disassembling.

Each day, there is less of us in the upstate New York house. Months before the movers arrive and haul our belongings over a thousand miles south, Katie and I begin to feel the house we've lived in for six years slowly slipping from us. Our moods shoot up and down. One moment we are driven, energy bursting from our ears, and the next we are crying or looking longingly at the empty shelves that once held Kipling, Whitman, Dickinson. The dogs are in a state of restlessness, wondering where their favorite toys are or the soft places for them to sleep. They sense our unease, our tension. One of them is always under our feet, the other one hides in corners. Our lives, for the moment, have been placed on hold. Our lives have become boxes and packing paper.

When moving, you live in a constant state of flux. The rhythm of the day is erratic. You wake up and pack. You stop living in the house. You end all dreams of a future here. You look ahead. Already, Katie and I think about our new home in Florida, imagining where we will place our bookshelves and framed art, our couch and television. What rooms will be our offices? Where should we place the bed? This is what gets us through the days. We are preparing our brains spatially, finding new spots for familiar items.

VIII

Despite my mother's new life in Thailand, she shipped all the furniture from our house in Chicago across the ocean. When I visit, her new house in Chiang Mai looks much the same as the house in Chicago. The black leather couches still face each other, and the same photos—mostly of me—dot the walls. In the kitchen, there's the same rice maker, the same dish scrubber in the sink. There's the same wooden chair and dresser in my bedroom. My mother uses the same pencils, with my high school and university insignia on them. She jots notes on the same yellow legal pad she used for at least twenty years (I've begun to think the damn thing is magical with its endless supply of paper). There are the same magnets on the refrigerator, including one of a cardinal—her favorite bird—frozen in flight.

IX

The birds are lost. For six years, we fed them. In the front yard, hung two suet feeders for the woodpeckers, a tube feeder filled with niger seeds for the finches and red polls, another feeder filled to the brim with sunflower seeds for cardinals and doves and blue jays, and a feeder of sugar water hanging off the eaves of the house for the hummingbirds.

When we took the feeders down, a day before we left for Florida, the birds came and flew to the empty places where the feeders were. The chickadees were loud with their complaints. The hummingbirds buzzed in and out. One goldfinch kept flying and flapping, flying and flapping, expecting to perch on a feeder. Watching the finch, I wondered if it still saw what was no longer there, wondered if they needed us, as much as we needed them. The birds had become accustomed to the food. It was what remained constant even during the worst of upstate winters. Now the feeders were gone, packed in boxes, headed to another part of the country.

"The thing about birds," Dinny once said to us when we were away from home and were worried about the birds, "is they always will find food. All they have to do is fly to other spots."

This is true with everything else.

We will find our usual spots again and again. We carry them with us—in our hearts, in our memories—wherever we move, and fly to them when we most need to.

III

There are no secrets in the world.

−Thai Proverb

Southside
Buddhist

- Working class ideology & attitude
- Southside me vs. smiling @ parties me
- who is he?
- embraces what society hates
- Fear of true self / acceptance

Southside Buddhist

Tough guys don't dance. You had better believe it.

–Norman Mailer

Genesis

The Southside me isn't a pleasant dude. He was born in a working class neighborhood in Chicago, among tough Polish and Irish. His father worked in a tile factory off Archer and could get Southside too, with a Thai accent. But you couldn't take him all that seriously because he was short and liked his slacks pressed and wore golfing polos. A Southsider needs nothing more than jeans and a T-shirt. If the winds get rough in the winter, a hoodie will do, or a denim jacket. A Southsider wears only gym shoes—dirty ones—so he can book it out of any situation. See ya.

When I was young, I got picked on a lot, a Peter Parker-type before he got bitten by the radioactive spider and started kickin' ass. For a while I took it. I buried all that hurt, that rage, inside, and there it sat building and building. Then one day, in third grade, the Southside me came out unexpectedly, like a Chicago gust. He unleashed himself on Dan Flavin, class clown, who had called his mom something not right earlier in the day. Rule 1: Don't ever mess with a Southsider's mom. People die for shit like that. So when Dan Flavin stood in line to go potty, the Southside me rabbit punched Dan Flavin in the back and watched Dan Flavin crumple to the ground. When the teacher asked what happened, Dan Flavin pointed at the Southside me, but I transformed back to the goody-goody everyone knew; the teacher didn't believe a word Dan Flavin said.

But that punch—it felt good, you know? It felt like the Southside me could fuck anything up. So, at nine, he enrolled in Tae Kwon Do and got a black belt. He studied Muay Thai at temple, though he despised the other students, a bunch of Sally Northsiders, a bunch of doctors' brats. He watched boxing and practiced his jab and right hook against walls; no joke. Made his knuckles callused and hard. The Southside me was getting himself well-versed in the fine arts of terminating, even though he was Buddhist, and as a Buddhist he shouldn't hurt an ant. He fucked ants up though, by the mound, and it didn't matter what his mom said—the thing about coming back as an ant in the next life—because the Southside me, he believed only in the moment; he was never seconds ahead of himself.

Secret Identity

Most of the time, I'm quiet. I smile. I listen. I'm the guy who manages to say nothing and remain memorable, like it or not. It is not an act, I assure you. It is residue from a past I'm still trying to piece together. Why is it I seek the back of room? Why is it in large social gatherings I feel trapped? I was a shy and anxious boy, but some of that sifted away, and what is left are these particles I cling to.

Most of the time, this is the person everyone sees. The gentle fat man. I am cordial to strangers, quick to say hello in the hallways of work, and like to leave presents for people just because. It is not an act, I assure you. It is, at times, a hindrance. Moments when the other me is needed, he doesn't come out. He stays in his cave, and I find myself smiling and apologizing too often.

Most of the time, I preoccupy myself with frivolous things, like my image. It's not an act, I assure you. I dress well—sporting nice long-sleeved shirts and stylish jeans. I wear hip black-rimmed glasses—Versace—and sport different types of hats—the fedora, the Kangol cap. I'm obsessive when it comes to shoes. I own at least thirty pairs and each is coordinated with an outfit.

Most of the time, everyone describes me as nice. I like the simplicity of the word, though my wife always says, "Before I met you, everyone considered me the nice one." At this I laugh and think, *They don't know the whole truth, do they?*

Talk the Talk

A Southsider doesn't finish the ending of his words, doesn't enunciate his consonants, and often times mumbles. He ends his sentences with questions, you know? His voice dwells in his throat, and his mouth barely opens when he speaks. A Southsider shortens everything. He doesn't like Ira; he prefers I or Suke. He has mastered the word "fuck": "That Sally, fuck"; "What a fuckin' D-bag,"; "Stupid, fuck-o." On average, every third word is "fuck." It's the clearest word in a sentence, a word that has a variety of meanings depending on inflection and body language. "Fuck you" with a laugh means "Are you kidding me?" "Fuck you" with a stiff pat on the back means "I love you." "Fuck you" in the lowest of tones means "I'm gonna kill you." That's another word a Southsider doesn't take lightly—"kill." We don't joke about it.

Once when my wife and I first dated, she said she'd kill me in jest.

I didn't know how to respond, so I didn't. But there must have been a look on my face. Of confusion, of fear. I could feel the hair on my neck rise. The last time someone said that to me, the Southsider came out and had to bump a few heads before someone broke the skirmish up. But here was this long-haired woman from the prairie, this poet, and I was falling for her.

"I'm kidding," she said. "My family says it all time."

"Oh."

"It's part of our language."

"Oh."

"I love you," she says.

And if there's another word a Southsider fears, even more

than "kill," then it's this one, "love." Another four letters, sharp like a blade.

Landscape

The Southside me is like the Southside neighborhoods with the cracked and weedy sidewalks, the eroding brown brick buildings, the abandoned factories. The Southside resists any type of change, unless it's for the worse. Ask my father who was laid off after twenty years. Ask my friends, who are still there, trying hard to make something for themselves. Ask the closed down industries. But amid the deterioration, there exists loyalty. It's like a tiny flower sprouting in a mound of shit.

Who Are You?

In my junior year of high school, I had an English teacher who challenged students with wit, sarcasm, and difficult questions. I don't remember her name, but I remember reading a lot of slave narratives and Native American literature. I also remember the pointed scowl she gave smartass students to shut them up, which usually worked, a miracle considering she taught a bunch of insubordinate Southside kids who would rather be anywhere else in the world but in an Early American literature class.

I sat with a group of guys who sat next to the cutest girls in the class, and I watched my friends pass notes back and forth, the girls giggling each time they read what the guys wrote.

Once this teacher—I think her last name began with a B— snatched one of the notes in transit and read it aloud.

"You're telling me this is more important than *A Light in August?*" Ms. B said. She carefully unraveled the note, her pinkies pointing up. Her glasses dangled around her neck, but she never put them on. She lifted them up and squinted, peering through them like a magnifying glass.

"How did you get out of the third grade, Mr. Wolfe, with handwriting like yours?"

Brian Wolfe—B-Bear—wasn't fazed. He was cocky like all Southsiders and liked the attention. Smiling, he said, "My mom says the same thing."

Ms. B ambled to the front of the room. She always carried the demeanor of a woman not from this time period, but one who strolled along the Seine in Paris with a parasol. "Well, isn't this the question of the class. I had hoped we could discuss this today in light of our readings. What Mr. Wolfe has written so sloppily to Ms. Styx is: *I would like to know you better.*"

The class laughed. B-Bear mouthed *I do* at Gina Styx, who was so red she hid her face in her arms.

"Hasn't it been the case this quarter," Ms. B said, "that all the texts we have read come back to the question of identity? Who are we? Where do we come from? To whom do we owe our roots?" Ms. B pointed at B-Bear. "Let's start with you, Mr. Wolfe. Please inform the class where your family originated."

"I'm all Irish, baby." Many in the class hooted.

Ms. B went around the room, asking each student where he or she came from, and to be precise. Most of the class said they were Italian, Polish, or Irish. There was a student whose parents were from Pakistan and grandparents were from India. An exchange student from Denmark said he wasn't Danish at all, but Swedish and German. A girl in the class said she had Indian blood, Cherokee, she thought, but she was mostly Mexican. Another said, "I'm everything that makes white, which is too much to list."

I dreaded the question. I was sixteen, and all I wanted to do was blend.

So when it was my turn to speak, I gave a smartass answer. "I'm a Chicagoan."

B-Bear patted my back and said, "Damn straight."

"Ira," Ms. B said. I was the only student she did not address with a formal title. "Be serious."

"A Southsider," I said.

"Hell yeah," B-Bear said.

"I am laughing on the inside," Ms. B said, her face without affect.

Later that semester, Ms. B told me during a conference that I was confused. On my papers, I wrote eloquent and insightful responses to the work we had read that semester. In class, I was a brainless twit. "Eventually, you'll have to choose." Ms. B put on her glasses for the first time and peered at me. "Which one will you be?"

Secret

The Southside me is not as tough as he thinks he is. He is, in fact, weak. He's power without a source. Don't tell him, though. It would destroy him.

Conflict

After nine years of marriage, my wife doesn't like the Southsider. She's from the sincere part of Illinois, where the tallest structures aren't skyscrapers but silos, where strangers could become friends in seconds, where physical confrontation is the last thing people want to be involved in. She knows when the Southsider has kidnapped her husband's body. She can tell by the tone of his voice, the half-smile that almost looks like a sneer. He comes out sometimes without notice or prelude. He's just there, an unwanted guest, and everything in his demeanor says cocky and unmotivated. Everything out of his mouth is sarcastic and insincere.

"What's wrong with you?" my wife says.

"Nothing."

"You're lying."

He doesn't look at her. He knows this woman can take him down with kindness. To look at her is to look at defeat.

"Something's up," she says. "You're acting weird."

It isn't weird to the Southsider. It simply is.

"Nothing," he says.

"You've been like this since morning."

"Like what?" And this is when he looks at her. With that smile. With that attitude. Like a challenge.

"Like this."

"I don't know what you're talking about." He really doesn't. Because to a Southsider, to admit something is wrong is to admit a flaw. A Southsider is not flawed.

"Don't talk to me until you're better," she says.

This usually does it. This wakes him up. And what follows, though he abhors it, is an apology.

Guilt

A Southsider can be from anywhere, not just Chicago. I've met some in upstate New York, in Florida, in Ohio. They usually hail from dying cities, like Cleveland, and Rochester, and Pittsburgh. They grew up in middle class families. Some of them, like me, have been far removed from their Southside roots, yet they can't fully shake the Southside out of them. They cling to that part of them like a security blanket. And if they do forget, even for a minute, guilt, heavy and suffocating, sits on their chest.

Lesson

At Sunday school, during Buddhism class, our *Ajahn*, monk teacher, told the story of Angulimala, a serial killer turned monk. I wasn't the best student. Usually, I sat in a corner of the room, doodling. This lesson, however, caught my attention. It was the detail of the severed thumbs that did it.

The tale of Angulimala was like most Buddhist parables: a man takes a wrong path and continues along this path because he feels he is far beyond saving. The path Angulimala was on was one of a murderer. As a young man, Angulimala's teacher, jealous of his student's virtuous nature, gave a false prophecy that if Angulimala didn't kill one thousand people, he would risk an early death. Out of his mind, Angulimala began slaying anyone who crossed his path. He cut off his victims' thumbs as a memorabilia, and at first, hung the thumbs on trees, but birds carried the thumbs away. For safekeeping, he began to wear the thumbs around his neck.

Years and years had gone by, and finally Angulimala need-ed one more victim to reach one thousand. He saw two peo-ple on the road—one was his mother (the Southsider's weak-ness!) and the other Buddha. He decided to kill Buddha, so he chased after him, his legs working hard on the dirt road, but he never gained ground. The harder Angulimala ran, the further he was from Buddha. It seemed improbable that a man who dashed at full speed could not catch a monk who walked.

"Yo, Monk," Angulimala said, panting, "What's up with you?"

Buddha turned to Angulimala, head glowing with wisdom, and said, "What do you mean?"

"Why don't you stop, so I can kill you?" Angulimala said, still winded.

"I have stopped, man," Buddha said. "You haven't."

These words saved Angulimala, of course, and he became a disciple of Buddha for the remainder of his life.

Afterwards, Ajahn said that most of us possessed a good and a bad, two identities intertwined in one body. Enlighten-ment is the merging of the two, which would lead to a deeper understanding of existence. What purpose, one should ask, does each identity serve?

Purpose? a Southsider would say. What the fuck?

In Buddhism, the purpose to life is to end suffering, just as Angulimala ended his after realizing his sins and adopting the Buddhist path. But the Southsider is in many ways the embodiment of suffering. He is a suffering boy, in a suffering neighborhood, in a suffering city, in a suffering country, in a suffering world. He is drowning in it.

Highlights

Once the Southside me emerged and wrote a letter to his Southside friends about how much he hated them; it was scathing in its delivery, prose littered with capital letters and exclamation points.

Once the Southside me emerged and pushed a kid so hard against a locker it dented.

Once the Southside me emerged and dirty danced the shit out of a blonde at a nightclub. After the dance he grabbed her face and kissed her. They never exchanged a word.

Once the Southside me emerged and rolled a bowling ball out of a minivan going sixty miles per hour. He wanted to test that physics law he learned at school.

Once the Southside me swung the car around mid-traffic to address a man he saw kick a dog. He didn't care about the car horns or dirty looks. He said to the man, "You kick that dog again, I will fuck your face up. Got me?"

Once the Southside me emerged and whipped a chair across a classroom because of a bad breakup. He was sent to see the school psychiatrist and commenced a forty-minute stare off, which he won.

Once the Southside me emerged and sat in front of his house on a lawn chair with a baseball bat and a bucket of golf balls. It was Halloween, and this Halloween he'd be damned if someone was going to fuck with the mailbox again.

Once the Southside me emerged and threw quarter sticks of dynamite out of his car in the Forest Preserves. Why? Because it was fun.

Once the Southside me emerged and crashed a Southside party with other Southsiders, and the Southside me delivered the best line of the night; when asked if he felt tough tonight, he said, "I'm tough every night."

The Good Side

The truth is the Southside me could be fun to be around. Find him at a party. Notice how the party gravitates around him. Listen to his laughter, a joyous sound. Watch how his face wears a permanent smile. During these moments he is not conscious of his deficiencies. He does not worry about what he looks like to others. He doesn't care what people say about him. He does not concern himself about being a good son, husband, friend, dog-father, writer, teacher, and all the other roles he plays. He simply exists. This is his most natural Buddhist state.

Aging

In the last few months, I've seen less and less of him. As I get older, so does he, and perhaps, he knows there's not much need for him anymore. He's not there when someone cuts me off or when the neighbor's house alarm goes off at six in the morning. I miss him, but I would never say it to his face. I miss him like how we miss our memories—a nostalgic longing, a yearning to have time back. I miss him in that he provided access to a rarely known side of me, and at times, it was liberating, despite the trouble he caused. Trouble can be, as he says, a source of comfort.

Now, he comes in those quiet times, baseball cap turned backwards in stone faded jeans and a *Just Do Me* T-shirt. He taps my shoulder. He nods. He says, "Yo." He says, "You forget about me?"

And I tell him in the sweetest voice I can muster, "How can I?"

Acknowledgments

Grateful acknowledgment is made to the following publications in which some of these essays appeared, some in slightly different versions:

The Briar Cliff Review: "Our Next Lives"
Brevity: A Journal of Concise Literary Nonfiction: "Chop Suey" and "The Cruelty We Delivered: An Apology"
Cold Mountain Review: "Constellations"
The Florida Review: "Wild Boys. Chicago Boys. Dumb Boys."
Indiana Review: "The Usual Spots"
Isotope: "Into the Country"
Juked: "Abridged Immigrant Narrative"
Make: "The In-between Time"
Nightsun: "The Take Over: A Love Story"
The Normal School: "Southside Buddhist."
The Pinch: "Tots-R-Us" and "To Kill a Thought: A Confession"
Shambhala Sun: "Please Don't Talk About It," "Playing with Buddha," and "Body Replies"
Sou'wester: "Floating Family"
Superstitious Review: "The Wide-Open Mouth"
Third Coast: "For the Novice Bird Watcher"

"Chop Suey" was reprinted in *Creative Nonfiction*'s Best of Brevity Issue.

"Our Next Lives" won *The Briar Cliff Review* Creative Nonfiction Contest and was a *Best American Essays* Notable.

"Into the Country" was a *Best American Essays* Notable.

"The Usual Spots" was a *Best American Essays* Notable.

About the Author

IRA SUKRUNGRUANG is the author of the memoir *Talk Thai: The Adventures of Buddhist Boy* and the coeditor of two anthologies on the topic of obesity: *What Are You Looking At? The First Fat Fiction Anthology* and *Scoot Over, Skinny: The Fat Nonfiction Anthology*. His first collection of poetry, *In Thailand It Is Night*, won the Anita Claire Scharf Award and was published by the University of Tampa Press in 2013. He is the recipient of the New York Foundation for the Arts Fellowship in Nonfiction Literature, an Arts and Letters Fellowship, and the Emerging Writer Fellowship. His work has appeared in many literary journals, including *Post Road, The Sun*, and *Creative Nonfiction*. He is one of the founding editors of *Sweet: A Literary Confection* (sweetlit.com) and teaches in the MFA program at the University of South Florida. For more information about him, please visit: www.sukrungruang.com.

About the Book

This book has been set in Adobe Garamond Pro types, developed from the sixteenth century roman types of Claude Garamond and the italics of Robert Granjon. Adobe Systems type designer Robert Slimbach visited the Plantin-Moretus Museum in Antwerp, Belgium, for research while working on the font. He later wrote, "The experience of studying near flawless proofs of Garamond's and Granjon's types was a revelation which led to a major overhaul of the working design." Slimbach's original digital fonts, released in 1989, have been further refined with digital options available in the newer Open Type format. The result is a versatile and highly readable serif face that preserves the grace and proportion of classical letterforms while projecting a timeless and contemporary clarity.

The cover of *Southside Buddhist* features an urban mural from the side of a Los Angeles car wash by street artists El Mac and Retna. The small photo on the back by University of Southern California Architecture and Fine Arts librarian Ruth Wallach shows the piece in context, with a commercial air dispenser and a parked car. The titling is the graffiti-like Ed Rogers font designed by Colin Kahn and Richard Kegler for P22 Type Foundry. The book was designed and typeset by Richard Mathews at the University of Tampa Press.